Dear DAVID:

Be Merry in God
or
Choose to be HAPPY!

I love you
honey
AlWAYS!
Merry Christmas
1999

Jane

The Saints Speak Today Series

Let Nothing Trouble You
St. Teresa of Avila
COMPILED BY HEIDI S. HESS

Restless Till We Rest in You
St. Augustine
COMPILED BY PAUL THIGPEN

A Dwelling Place Within
St. Francis of Assisi
COMPILED BY MARY VAN BALAN HOLT

Be Merry in God
St. Thomas More
COMPILED BY PAUL THIGPEN

THE SAINTS SPEAK TODAY

Be Merry in God

*60 Reflections From the
Writings of Saint Thomas More*

COMPILED BY
PAUL THIGPEN

CHARIS

SERVANT PUBLICATIONS
ANN ARBOR, MICHIGAN

Charis Books is an imprint of Servant Publications especially designed to serve Roman Catholics.

Scripture references, unless otherwise noted, have been taken from the Revised Standard Version of the Bible, © 1946, 1952, 1971 by the Division of Christian Education of the National Council of the Churches of Christ in the USA. Used by permission.

Servant Publications
P.O. Box 8617
Ann Arbor, MI 48107

Cover design: Left Coast Design, Portland, OR

99 00 01 02 10 9 8 7 6 5 4 3 2 1

LIBRARY OF CONGRESS CATALOGING-IN-PUBLICATION DATA

Be merry in God : 60 reflections from the writings of Saint Thomas More /
    compiled by Paul Thigpen.
        p. cm. —(The saints speak today)
    ISBN 1-56955-090-5 (alk. paper)
    1. Catholic Church Prayer-books and devotions—English. 2. Spiritual life—
Catholic Church. 3. Devotional calendars—Catholic Church. I. Thigpen,
Thomas Paul, 1954-   . II. More, Thomas, Sir, Saint, 1478-1535. Selections.
1999. III. Series.
BX2182.2.B36   1999
242—dc21   99-19445
                                                        CIP

Printed in the United States of America
ISBN 1-56955-090-5

For Dr. James Patrick, Provost, and the fellows,
students, staff, and friends of
The College of Saint Thomas More,
Fort Worth, Texas,
my dear colleagues who labor diligently and merrily
because they agree with the saint whose name they bear that
"learning joined with virtue" is to be preferred to
"all the treasures of kings."

Contents

"Diligent Labor ..." The Virtuous Life

"Dirt and Mire ..." Those Deadly Sins

I beseech our Lord to breathe into the reader's breast His Holy Spirit, who can teach him within his heart. Without Him, all that the mouths of all the world would be able to teach in men's ears would avail only little.

ST. THOMAS MORE,
A Dialogue of Comfort Against Tribulation

Introduction

Thomas More: The Merry Saint

The gold chain around Sir Thomas More's neck testified publicly to his position as one of England's most prominent statesmen. But beneath the chain, closer to his heart, lay a silent witness to a far higher vocation, a far richer treasure: Under the ruffles of Renaissance finery, he wore a hair shirt next to his skin. Endured as a secret penance—for years not even More's wife knew he wore it—that scratchy garment of animal hair scrubbed his soul and kept him from becoming too comfortable in a life that was as fragile as it was fraught with temptations.

The mighty Lord Chancellor of England behaving like an ascetic monk: What are we to make of such a paradox? Perhaps Jesus' words on the night He was betrayed offer us a clue to understanding such a man. The Lord prayed in that terrible hour in Gethsemane—a prayer More himself carefully pondered—that His disciples would be able to remain in the world without being of the world (see Jn 17:11-19). Early in life More had considered becoming a Carthusian, withdrawn from public life in the sweet labor of contemplation, but he had concluded that his vocation lay elsewhere. When we consider the remarkable gifts that he was later to employ on behalf of the Church and his country, we can only agree that his discernment was correct. More's intellectual brilliance, moral integrity, and religious faith were desperately needed in the tumultuous world of the Renaissance and Reformation. Yet that world did not own him; he belonged to another. Each prick of the hair shirt reminded him of that truth.

No doubt More faced ample worldly enticements. Born in London in 1478, the son of a lawyer and judge, he became acquainted early on with the perks of public service, and as a young page in the household of the archbishop of Canterbury he had the chance to observe closely the pleasures that wealth and status could afford. After schooling at Oxford and studying law at Lincoln's Inn, he was admitted to the bar in 1501 and embarked on an illustrious career that would be the envy of any politician.

More entered Parliament in 1504 and became undersheriff of London in 1510. Having tutored the little prince who would become Henry VIII, he was a favorite of the court once the young man took the throne. The king sent More as ambassador to France and Flanders, appointed him to the Royal Council in 1517, and knighted him in 1521. He was chosen speaker of the House of Commons in 1523, became High Steward of Cambridge in 1525, and four years later was appointed by the king as Lord Chancellor—one of the most powerful offices in the realm.

Though he could hardly be called extravagant, for most of his adult life More enjoyed the lifestyle of a man of some means: He owned multiple homes, barns, and lands; employed live-in servants and private tutors for his children; and collected exotic animals and artifacts as a hobby. His fine education and intellect afforded him as well what were, in his day, the quite rare pleasures of scholarship. His home was a center of Renaissance culture in England, and he himself was known throughout Europe as one of the leading scholars and intellectual figures of his day, translating Lucian from the Latin and writing poetry, history, political philosophy, religious treatises, devotional books, and prayers.

Status and wealth, power and fame: More had them all. He stood undeniably in the world. How could such a "worldly" man have become a saint? How did he avoid being of the world—or perhaps we should ask, how did he maintain a firm allegiance to the world to come?

We find in this man's life no single or easy strategy for sainthood. Yet we see a pattern in his words and in his deeds: Through one means or another, More continually exposed the shadowy nature of this world by turning upon it the brilliant light of eternity. He was able to maintain persistently his allegiance to the world to come in large measure because that world was incessantly before his eyes, more real to him in many ways than the worldly temptations that surrounded him. Such a vision prompted him, for example, to have his own tomb built and his epitaph engraved during the prime of his life: a stark reminder of his own mortality.

Other illustrations of this otherworldly perspective abound throughout his life. No doubt the daily routine of a household as large, wealthy, and prominent as his included a thousand distractions from spiritual priorities. Yet More found ways to focus on what was most important: He led his family and servants each evening in their prayers. He had Scripture and scriptural commentaries read aloud at mealtimes, followed by family discussion of the texts. He devoted his Fridays to prayer and study. And he insisted that no business would ever keep the household from church on Sundays and other days when they were obliged to be at Mass. Once while in church he even refused to answer the king's summons until the Mass was over—making it clear whose command took priority.

The hair shirt was only one of More's personal austerities. He was known to discipline himself with other, equally private, penances, such as sleeping on planks with a log for a pillow (and allowing himself only four or five hours of sleep a night). He dressed as simply as possible when his public duties did not require otherwise—he was not fond of that gold chain, nor the ruffled shirts—and when he did have to be decked out in finery, he wore it with such carelessness that his family was embarrassed and his acquaintances joked about his appearance. Though he spread many a banquet for family and friends, he often turned down delicacies at the table for himself. The forms of gambling so popular among his wealthy contemporaries he banished from his home.

One sad incident recorded in his correspondence reflects how lightly he held his possessions. Fire one day consumed his barns, and the grain that filled them, while he was out of town on business. When he received from his distraught wife a letter telling him of the terrible misfortune, his letter of reply showed no tinge of self-pity or bitterness. "Be of good cheer," he told her, "and take all the household with you to church, where you should thank God: both for what He has given us and for what He has left us.... I pray you: With the children and with all the household, be merry in God."[1] With an eye on eternity, More could own barns, grain, and everything else without their owning him.

Those who were close to More often learned a lesson or two from him in this regard. Anne Cresacre, his daughter-in-law, once begged him to buy her a string of pearls. Hoping to remind her of the vanity of such costly trinkets, he gave her instead a string of white peas. The strategy worked, and she longed for expensive jewelry no more.

More's focus on spiritual values rather than transient possessions was evidenced as well by his persistent works of mercy and justice. The poor were frequently invited to his table, and he established an almshouse to share his wealth. He gave litigants free advice about how to resolve their differences without his services, and he refused all gifts from those who might try to buy his influence.

The allurements of power and status were similarly repulsed by More's belief in the fragility of life, a conviction clearly reflected in a brief exchange with his son-in-law (and later biographer), William Roper. One evening King Henry dropped in unexpectedly for dinner at More's home at Chelsea. After much merriment, His Majesty walked with his host in the garden for about an hour with his arm around the older man's neck. After the king had left for home, Roper, exuberant about the evening, remarked to More that he had rarely seen Henry favor anyone in that way.

More agreed, but added soberly, "Even so, I have no cause to be proud of it. For if my head would win him a castle in France, it should not fail to go."[2]

The saint's last public words, uttered on the scaffold in 1535 when Henry had in fact decided to exchange More's head for political advantage, sum up well the kind of vision he had maintained during his lifetime: "I die the king's servant," he reminded his listeners, "but God's first." The king's servant— in the world. But God's first—not of the world.[3]

Like his deeds, More's writings maintain this sharp focus on the life to come. The somber treatise on *The Last Things*, for example, centers on the "four last things" of classical Catholic theology: death, judgment, hell, and heaven. In this treatise More shows how a serious consideration of our ultimate destiny can serve as effective "medicine" to cure spiritual sickness. The traditional "deadly sins" are analyzed carefully here; More seems to have known from personal experience how powerfully these sins can grip a soul. Nevertheless, as he insists, we need only remember how fleeting are those things that serve as the occasions for our pride or envy, our avarice or gluttony, to break their hold on us. And recalling that we will one day give a full account for our deeds can chasten the way we live today.

This book, perhaps his most sobering, may seem at times like the grim reflections of a man on his deathbed, where most people at last (if ever) take their mortality seriously. Yet it came from his pen when he was near the height of his rise to power and prestige in the king's service. No matter how alluring the gold and the glory, the wine, women, and song of Henry's court, More was able to keep his distance by taking the long view of things. The worms, he never tired of repeating, will one day have it all.

If such were his thoughts in the prime of his life, how grave must they have been when at last his integrity brought him into conflict with his old friend Henry. More was imprisoned and threatened with disembowelment—the horrible form of execution reserved for traitors—when he refused to recognize the king's claim that he could declare himself the supreme head of the church in England. For fifteen months he languished in the shadow of the scaffold, and in those terrible days he wrote some of his finest works: his treatises *To Receive the Blessed Body of Our Lord, On the Sadness of Christ,* and *On the Passion;* his *Dialogue of Comfort Against Tribulation;* and his collection of final instructions, meditations, and prayers.

Even so, when compared to *The Last Things,* there is at times a freedom, even a lightness, in these later works—the *Dialogue,* for example, is filled with "merry tales." Yet this quality in itself bears testimony to his convictions about eternity. Once the die was cast, the career crucified, the world and all its enticements surrendered, More was able to soar merrily above the horrors of the moment to behold the promise of glory that awaited him if only he could persevere to the end.

Such lightness, though a recurrent theme throughout More's life, startled his contemporaries—as it does ours—when it appeared one last bright time as the saint joked with his executioners. Weary and stumbling from long ill-treatment, and with his hands tied behind his back, he feared that he might not be able to negotiate the shaky steps up to the scaffold to be beheaded. So he turned to the lieutenant beside him and said, "I pray you, see me safely up, and for my coming down let me shift for myself." Once he had laid his head on the block, he asked the executioner to wait while he moved aside his beard, which had grown long and scraggly during his imprisonment. After all, he quipped, his beard had never committed any treason![4]

These were only the last of many jests from a man who had persistently taken his own advice to "be merry in God." For More was from his early days a first-class joker. As a boy he once wrote a stand-up comedy routine to be recited as a welcome to the guests at a feast. His youthful Latin compositions play on the fact that his name in Greek—Moros—means fool, and they sparkle with wit: "If your feet were as light as your head," one noted, "you could outrun a hare!"[5]

As an adult he became famous well beyond England for his practical jokes, such as "medicating" the food of guests—with what kind of surprises, we can only speculate with glee. Even his formal treatises include a number of stories whose good humor can still draw laughter nearly five centuries later. And though he may have taught his children that "virtue and learning are meat," while "play is only the sauce," the children well knew that he considered the spice of the sauce indispensable.[6]

Is it any wonder that such a man's household included a live-in professional jester and a pet monkey?

Here again, More presents us with a paradox: How could the author of *The Sadness of Christ,* the man who wrote so much about the deadly sins, about death, judgment, and hell, be at the same time such a "merry saint"?

Perhaps we need to reconsider the relations between hope and humor. Someone once said that God has given us hope to encourage us about what we can one day become, and humor to console us for what we are now. Laughter is, after all, our response to the gap between what is and what should be. A finely tuned sense of humor is therefore often the distinguishing mark of clear vision—the kind that sees this life sharply with all its incongruities, yet sees as well the possibilities and implications that lie hidden beneath the surface. Thomas More had such a vision.

The key here, it seems, lies in the last two words of the saint's exhortation: "Be merry *in God.*" Without God—without the hope of another world beyond this one, for which this one is longing—there could be no true merriment. There could be only the shallow giggle of flippancy, or the hollow mockery of the cynic. To be truly merry is to live lightly in this world, to be unburdened with cares about things that are quickly passing away. In a sense, we might say that for those who take God and His will with appropriate seriousness, nothing else need be taken seriously. To be in the world but not of the world is, among other things, to laugh at the world.

And so Saint Thomas More, enduring the ordinary trials we all suffer, and a few more extraordinary ones besides, remained merry for a lifetime, and he called all those around him to merriment as well. Even in his last letter, written on the eve of his execution, the words ring like the crescendo of a musical refrain that has sounded through all his correspondence: "Be merry in God!" When you lose a loved one, be merry. When the barns burn, be merry. When your career is shattered, when your friends betray you, when you end up in prison, when death stares you in the face—"Be merry in God!" Today's tears, he reminds us all, can water the soil of our souls, and one day "we will have in heaven a merry, laughing harvest forever!"[7]

After all, we must never forget that heaven is the last of "the four last things."

Paul Thigpen

"That Life-Giving Grace..."

SCRIPTURE AND SACRAMENT

DAY 1
Scripture and Faith

But as for you, continue in what you have learned and have firmly believed, knowing from whom you learned it and how from childhood you have been acquainted with the sacred writings which are able to instruct you for salvation through faith in Christ Jesus.

2 TIMOTHY 3:14-15

MORNING READING

Unless a man first believes that the Holy Scriptures are the word of God, and that the word of God is true, how can he take any consolation in what the Scripture tells him? A man will necessarily gain little fruit from the Scripture, if he either fails to believe that it is the word of God, or else thinks that even though it is, it still cannot be trusted. The comforting words of Scripture help a man only to the extent that this faith is strong. And no man can give to himself nor to anyone else this virtue of faith. By preaching men may be ministers to encourage faith, and the man who with his own free will obeys the inward inspiration of God can be a weak coworker with God Almighty Himself; yet such faith is indeed still the gracious gift of God Himself. Therefore, feeling the symptoms of a faith that is quite faint, let us pray to Him who gives it that it may please Him to help and increase it.

Instructed in Thy holy law, to praise Thy word I lift my voice;
O Lord, be Thou my present help, for Thy commandments are
my choice.
For Thy salvation I have longed, and in Thy law is my delight;
Enrich my soul with life divine, and help me by Thy judgments
right.

FROM THE PSALTER, 1912 (from Psalm 19)

FOR REFLECTION

"Men are so weak in themselves as they try to walk the way that leads to life, that no man can come to Christ unless the Father first comes to him, and takes him by the hand, and even pulls him along." Father, increase my faith!

EVENING READING

Let us not allow the strength and fervor of our faith to grow lukewarm (or, I should say, ice cold), and to lose its strength by scattering our minds abroad over so many trivial things that we rarely think about spiritual matters. We should collect our thoughts from the distractions of worldly fantasies, and thus gather our faith together into a narrow little room. Then, like the tiny grain of the mustard seed, which by nature easily germinates, we should plant this faith in the garden of our soul, with all weeds pulled up so that our faith can better feed. Then it will grow, and spread up so high, that the birds—that is, the holy angels in heaven—will breed in our soul to bring forth virtues in the branches of our faith. And then with the faithful trust that we will put in God's promise through a true belief in His word, we will be well able to command a great mountain of tribulation to disappear from the place where it stands in our heart.

The Scripture, Simple Yet Profound

All scripture is inspired by God and profitable for teaching, for reproof, for correction, and for training in righteousness, that the man of God may be complete, equipped for every good work.
2 TIMOTHY 3:16-17

MORNING READING

By the secret counsel of the Holy Spirit, the Scriptures have been crafted in such a way that they are plain and simple enough for every man to find in them what he needs to understand. Yet again, they are so lofty and difficult, no man is so cunning that he won't find there things far beyond his reach, things far too deep to fathom.

As a good, holy saint once said, the Scriptures are so marvelously made that even though a mouse can wade in them, an elephant can also drown there.

Oh, may these heavenly pages be my ever-dear delight,
And still new beauties may I see, and still increasing light.
Divine Instructor, gracious Lord, be Thou forever near,
Teach me to love Thy sacred Word, and find my Savior there.
ANNE STEELE, 1716–78

FOR REFLECTION

"Good Lord, give us Your grace not to hear with our ears nor read with our eyes this Gospel as if it were a mere pastime, but instead let it sink into our hearts with such compassion that it will lead to the everlasting profit of our souls."

EVENING READING

No matter how lowly a man may be, if he will seek his way through the Scripture with the staff of faith in his hand; and hold that staff, and search out his way with it; and have the holy, ancient teachers of the Church for his guides as well; making his way with good intentions and a lowly heart; using reason and refusing no good learning; calling on God for wisdom, grace and help that he may keep his way and follow his good guides; then he will never fall into danger, but will wade through surely and well. And he will come to the end of his journey at the place for which he was searching.

Reading the Scripture With the Church

First of all you must understand this, that no prophecy of scripture is a matter of one's own interpretation, because no prophecy ever came by the impulse of man, but men moved by the Holy Spirit spoke from God.

2 PETER 1:20-21

MORNING READING

God's precepts will never be obeyed if every man may boldly devise for himself a conscience based on a commentary on God's Word that he has crafted himself according to his own fantasies. For in this matter—in which people justify following their own way against the commandment of God by appealing to their private devotions—these words of the Scripture are proved true: "There is a way that seems right to man, but its end leads to hell" [Prv 14:12].

For example, King Saul thought, according to his own understanding, that he did very well when he kept and spared the goodly oxen for sacrifice [see 1 Sm 15:1-23]. But when by doing so he broke the commandment of God to put to death all the animals in the conquered town, this falsely contrived devotion did not help him, but actually cost him his kingdom.

We praise Thee for the radiance that from the hallowed page,
A lantern to our footsteps, shines on from age to age.
The Church from Thee, her Master, received the gift divine,
And still that light she lifteth o'er all the earth to shine.
O make Thy Church, dear Savior, a lamp of purest gold,
To bear before the nations Thy true light as of old.

WILLIAM WALSHAM HOW, 1823–97

FOR REFLECTION

"If a man will not take the teachings of the Catholic faith as a rule of interpretation when he studies the Scripture—but instead, being distrustful, studies the Scripture to find out whether or not the faith of the Church is true—he cannot fail to fall into errors." Lord, teach me to read the Scripture in the light of the faith of the Church.

EVENING READING

King Saul should not have followed his own understanding in the matter of sparing the oxen, but should have asked the prophet by whom God's precept had come to him. In the same way, if a man should doubt the knowledge and understanding of anything written in the Scripture, he is not wise then to take upon himself the authority to interpret, boldly depending on his own mind. Instead, he should depend on the interpretation of the holy teachers and the saints of old, and on the interpretation that has been received and allowed by the universal Church. For it was the Church through which the Scripture has come into our hands and been delivered to us in the first place, and without the Church, as Saint Augustine says, we could not know which books were Holy Scripture.

The Mysteries of the Scripture

O the depth of the riches and wisdom and knowledge of God!
How unsearchable are his judgments and how inscrutable his
ways!

ROMANS 11:33

MORNING READING

It certainly appears clear to me that no one understands the
sense of all scriptural texts so fully that he does not still find
hidden there many mysteries that are yet to be understood—
such as passages about the times of the Antichrist or the last
judgment by Christ, which are things that will remain hidden
until Elijah returns to explain them [see Mal 4:5]. So it seems
to me that I can rightly apply to holy Scripture this exclamation
of the apostle about the wisdom of God, for it is in the
Scripture that God has laid up the vast treasures of His
wisdom.

Break Thou the bread of life, dear Lord, to me,
As Thou didst break the loaves beside the sea;
Beyond the sacred page I seek Thee, Lord;
My spirit pants for Thee, O living Word!

MARY A. LATHBURY, 1841–1913

FOR REFLECTION

"If any biblical text seems to us contrary to any point of the Church's faith and belief, we should be certain that there is either some error by the translator, or by the printer—or perhaps some hindrance or another keeps us from understanding it aright." Holy Spirit, help me to trust that Your words are true even when I cannot understand them fully.

EVENING READING

Nevertheless, these days there are showing up, first in one place and then in another, much like swarms of bees or hornets, those who boast that they are "self-taught." They claim that without the commentaries of the holy teachers of old, they are able to discover as clear, open, and easy all those things that all the ancient fathers confessed they found quite difficult. Yet the fathers were men of no less talent, training, or tireless zeal than these moderns. And as for that "spirit" to which these moderns give such lip service yet rarely have in their hearts, in this regard the fathers far surpassed them just as they did in holiness of life. But now these modern men, who have sprouted up overnight as "theologians" claiming to know everything, not only dispute the interpretation of Scripture offered by all those men who led such heavenly lives; they even fail to agree among themselves about the great dogmas of the Christian faith! Rather, each of them, whoever he may be, claiming that he has the truth, vanquishes the rest—only to be vanquished by the rest in turn. But they all are alike in this way: They all oppose the Catholic faith, and they all are conquered by it.

Reason and Faith

Gird up your minds.

1 PETER 1:13a

MORNING READING

Whoever would grasp what he must believe must use reason. Yet reason must not resist faith, but rather walk with her, waiting on her as her handmaid. And even though at times reason seems contrary to faith, yet in truth faith never gets along without her. But just as a handmaid who loses all restraint, or gets drunk, or grows too proud, will then chatter too much and argue with her mistress, and act sometimes as if she were insane, in the same way, reason—if it is allowed to run riot and lift up its heart in pride—will not fail to rebel against her mistress, faith. On the other hand, if she is brought up well, and guided well, and kept in good temper, she will never disobey faith because she will be in her right mind. Therefore, let your powers of reason be well trained, for surely faith never gets along without her.

God be in my head, and in my understanding;
God be in mine eyes, and in my looking;
God be in my mouth, and in my speaking;
God be in my heart, and in my thinking.

SARUM PRIMER, 1558

FOR REFLECTION

"I would rather have learning joined with virtue than all the treasures of kings." Lord, grant me the grace to discipline my mind so that it will be of service to You.

EVENING READING

Now in the study of Scripture—in deciphering the meaning, in considering what you read, in pondering the purpose of various commentaries, in comparing diverse texts that seem contrary, even though they are not—I don't deny that the most important thing is to have grace and God's special help. But at the same time, He uses man's reason as an instrument as well. God also helps us to eat—but not without our mouth! Now just as the hand becomes more nimble through experience, and the legs and feet are more swift and sure through practice in running, and the whole body is more invigorated by some kind of exercise, no doubt in the same way reason is made more lively by the labor and exercise of logic, philosophy, and other liberal arts. The power of judgment is well ripened through these disciplines as well as through reading the laws and stories of orators. And even though many men consider poetry nothing more than painted words, yet it helps the power of judgment considerably, and makes a man, among other things, well furnished with one special thing—without which all learning is half lame: a good natural intelligence.

DAY 6
Confession Before Communion

Let a man examine himself, and so eat of the bread and drink of the cup.

1 CORINTHIANS 11:28

MORNING READING

Therefore we have great cause, with great dread and reverence, to consider well the state of our own soul when we go to the table of God. As far as we can, with the help of His special grace, diligently prayed for beforehand, we must purge and cleanse our souls by confession, contrition, and penance, fully intending to forsake from then on the proud desires of the devil; the greedy covetousness of wretched, worldly wealth; and the foul inclinations of the filthy flesh. We must fully intend to persevere and continue in the ways of God and in holy cleanness of spirit.

Depth of mercy! Can there be mercy still reserved for me?
Can my God His wrath forbear—me, the chief of sinners, spare?
I have long withstood His grace, long provoked Him to His face,
Would not hearken to His calls, grieved Him by a thousand falls.
Now incline me to repent; let me now my sins lament;
Now my foul revolt deplore, weep, believe, and sin no more.

CHARLES WESLEY, 1707–88

FOR REFLECTION

"Forgive me those sins which through my own fault, through evil inclinations and evil habits, I cannot recognize as sin because my reason has become so blinded by sensuality. And illumine, good Lord, my heart, and give me Your grace to know these sins and to acknowledge them; and forgive me the sins I have forgotten through negligence, and bring them to my mind with grace so that I might confess them rightly."

EVENING READING

We may not go rashly to God's table, but at a suitable time beforehand we must consider well and examine surely the state in which our soul stands. In this regard it will be not only quite hard, but perhaps even impossible, through our own diligence alone to attain a full certainty about the state of our soul without some special revelation from God. For as the Scripture says: "No man living knows whether he is worthy of the favor or hatred of God" [Eccl 9:1]. Nevertheless, in this matter God, because of His great goodness, is content if we are as diligent as possible to see that we are not disposed to commit any mortal sin.

Despite all our diligence, God—whose eye pierces much more deeply to the bottom of our heart than our own eye does—may see within us some kind of sin that we cannot see there ourselves. As Saint Paul said: "I am not conscious of anything against me, but I do not thereby stand acquitted" [1 Cor 4:4]. Even so, because of His great bounty, God accepts our true diligence in searching our heart to such an extent that He does not charge us with any sin that lurks secretly there in a way that would make us unworthy to receive this Blessed Sacrament. Instead, the strength and virtue of that sacrament purges and cleanses us from such sin.

DAY 7
Making Penance Fruitful

For the moment all discipline seems painful rather than pleasant; later it yields the peaceful fruit of righteousness to those who have been trained by it.

HEBREWS 12:11

MORNING READING

A penitent begins to profit and grow in grace and the favor of God when he feels a pleasure and quickening in his labor and pain taken in prayer, almsgiving, pilgrimage, fasting, discipline, tribulation, affliction, and other such spiritual exercises. By these the soul willingly works with the body for their own chastisement, to purge and rub out the rusty, tarnished spots with which sin has defiled them in the sight of God, leaving fewer to be burned out in the fire of purgatory. And when, as I say, a man feels in this pain a pleasure, he has a token of great grace that his penance is pleasing to God.

Jesus, the sinner's friend, to Thee, lost and undone, for aid I flee,
Weary of earth, myself and sin: Open Thine arms, and take me in.
Pity and heal my sin-sick soul; 'tis Thou alone canst make me whole:
Dark, till in me Thine image shine, and lost, I am, till Thou art mine.

CHARLES WESLEY, 1707–88

FOR REFLECTION

"The Church has always taught that all our penance without Christ's passion is not worth a pea."

EVENING READING

As the holy Scripture says, our Lord loves a cheerful giver [see 2 Cor 9:7]. On the other hand, when one does the spiritual business of penance, not cheerfully, but with a dullness of spirit and weariness of mind, he works twice as much and suffers four times as much pain, since his bodily pain is not relieved by spiritual rejoicing or comfort. I will not say that his labor is lost, but I dare be bold to say, that he profits much less with much more pain. For certain it is, that the best souls, and those that have best travailed in spiritual business, find the most comfort in it.

True Body and True Blood

For any one who eats and drinks without discerning the body eats and drinks judgment upon himself.

1 CORINTHIANS 11:29

MORNING READING

In this testing and examination of ourselves before we approach God's table, one very special point to observe is to test and examine whether we hold the right faith and belief concerning that holy Blessed Sacrament itself: namely, that we truly believe that it is, as indeed it is, under the form and likeness of bread, the true blessed Body, Flesh and Blood of our holy Savior Christ Himself. We must believe that it is the very same Body and the very same Blood that died and was shed on the cross for our sin; and gloriously rose again to life on the third day; and—with the souls of holy saints fetched out of hell—ascended and climbed up marvelously into heaven; and sits there at the right hand of the Father; and will visibly descend in great glory to judge the living and the dead; and will reward all men according to their works.

Godhead here in hiding whom I do adore,
Masked by these bare shadows, shape and nothing more.
See, Lord, at Thy service, low lies here a heart
Lost, all lost, in wonder at the God Thou art.

ST. THOMAS AQUINAS, 1225–74;
TRANSLATED BY GERARD MANLEY HOPKINS, 1844–89

FOR REFLECTION

"If a man can believe that the Eucharist is Christ's very body and yet still not be inflamed to receive Him devoutly in it, how much more likely is a man to receive this Blessed Sacrament quite coldly and without devotion if he doesn't even believe it is truly His Body—but thinks it is a mere token of Him instead?" Lord, give me faith to receive Your true Body and Blood in the Eucharist.

EVENING READING

We must see to it that we firmly believe that this Blessed Sacrament is not merely a sign, or a type, or a token of that holy Body of Christ. Rather, we must believe that it is—in perpetual remembrance of the bitter passion He suffered for us—the very same precious Body of Christ that suffered by His own almighty power and inexpressible goodness, now consecrated and given to us. This point of belief is of such necessity and importance in the reception of this Blessed Sacrament by those who are old enough to understand it that, without such belief, they clearly receive the sacrament to their damnation. And that one point, if believed very fully and firmly, should be enough to move any man to receive the sacrament well in every other regard. For note well the words of Saint Paul on the matter: "For anyone who eats of this bread and drinks of this cup unworthily eats and drinks judgment on himself, in that he does not discern the Body of our Lord" [see 1 Cor 11:27-29].

Reverence for the Eucharist

Lift up your heads, O gates! and be lifted up, O ancient doors! that the King of glory may come in. Who is this King of glory? The Lord of hosts, he is the King of glory!

PSALM 24:9-10

MORNING READING

But now, having our full faith in this point firmly grounded—that what we receive is the true blessed Body of Christ—I trust we will not really need any further instruction to teach us, or any further exhortation to stir and excite us to receive Him with all humility and reverence. For we must only consider: What if there were a great ruler of the world who, because of some special favor toward us, chose to come visit us in our own house? What a fuss we would then make, and what a work it would be for us to see that our house was put in good order in every regard to the best of our ability. And we would hope that by having everything so well provided and ordered, such an honorable reception would demonstrate to him what affection we bear him and in what high estimation we hold him. Now compare that worldly prince and this heavenly Prince—two princes who have less in common than a man and a mouse! In this light, we should inform and teach ourselves what a lowly mind, what a tender, loving heart, what a reverent, humble manner we ourselves should endeavor to have as we receive this glorious heavenly King, the King of all kings, almighty God Himself, who so lovingly condescends not only to enter into our house, but to allow His precious Body into our vile, wretched carcass, and His Holy Spirit into our poor simple soul.

Jesus, my Lord, my God, my all! How can I love Thee as I ought?

And how revere this wondrous Gift so far surpassing hope or thought?

Thy Body, Soul and Godhead, all! O mystery of love divine!

I cannot compass all I have, for all Thou hast and art is mine.

Sound, then, His praises higher still, and come, ye angels, to our aid;

For this is God, the very God, who has both men and angels made.

FREDERICK FABER, 1814–63

FOR REFLECTION

"Then when we come to His holy table, into the presence of His blessed Body, let us consider His high and glorious majesty, which His great goodness hides from us there." Help me see your majesty in the Eucharist, Jesus, with the eyes of faith.

EVENING READING

What diligence can be sufficient for us here, what attentive care can we judge to be enough, to prepare for the coming of this almighty King—coming as so special a gracious favor, not at our expense, not to spend our wealth, but to enrich us with His wealth? And to think that He comes after all the times we have terribly displeased Him, and acted so ungratefully in return for so many of the incomparable benefits He had given us! How we should labor now and make provisions so that the house of our soul—which God is coming to rest in—will have no poisoned spider or cobweb of mortal sin hanging in the roof! How we should sweep away even so much as a straw or a feather of a trivial bad thought spied on the floor!

Receiving the Eucharist Worthily

Whoever, therefore, eats the bread or drinks the cup of the Lord in an unworthy manner will be guilty of profaning the body and blood of the Lord.

1 CORINTHIANS 11:27

MORNING READING

Those who receive the Eucharist unworthily receive it in a merely sacramental way. For they truly receive the very Body and Blood of our Savior into their body in the Blessed Sacrament. For as Saint Augustine says of the false traitor Judas, even though he was wicked and received the sacrament on Maundy Thursday to his damnation, yet it was nevertheless truly our Lord's Body that he received. But those who receive the Eucharist in mortal sin do not receive it spiritually; that is, they do not receive the spiritual reality of the sacrament. Whoever receives it in mortal sin, even though he receives Christ's holy flesh into his body, he does not receive Christ's Holy Spirit into His soul.

O Lord, I am not worthy that Thou shouldst come to me:
But speak the word of comfort, my spirit healed shall be.
And humbly I'll receive Thee, the Bridegroom of my soul,
No more by sin to grieve Thee, or fly Thy sweet control.
Increase my faith, dear Jesus, in Thy real presence here,
And make me feel most deeply that Thou to me art near.

PROBABLY BASED ON
"O HERR, ICH BIN NICHT WUERDIG,"
LANDSHUTER GESANGBUCH, 1777

FOR REFLECTION

"Make us all, good Lord, truly participants of that Holy Sacrament this day, and every day make us all living members, sweet Savior Christ, of Your holy mystical body, Your Catholic Church."

EVENING READING

Because of His great sovereign patience, God does not refuse to enter bodily into the vile bodies of those whose filthy minds refuse to receive Him into their souls through divine grace. For then, such people receive Him sacramentally and not truly: that is, they receive His very blessed Body into theirs under the sacramental sign, but they do not receive the thing to which that sign points, namely, its virtue and effect. Instead of that life-giving grace—that grace by which they should be incorporated as living members in Christ's holy mystical body—instead they receive their judgment and their damnation.

The Divine Humility

I am the living bread which came down from heaven; if any one eats of this bread, he will live for ever; and the bread which I shall give for the life of the world is my flesh.

JOHN 6:51

MORNING READING

Those who receive the Blessed Sacrament in due manner and worthily are those who receive the blessed Body of our Lord both sacramentally and truly. When I say "worthily," I don't mean that any man is so good, or can be so good, that his goodness could make him of right and reason worthy to receive into his lowly, earthly body that holy, blessed, glorious flesh and blood of almighty God Himself, with His heavenly soul in it, and with the majesty of His eternal Godhead. I mean instead that such a man can prepare himself, working with the grace of God, to stand in such a condition so that the incomparable goodness of God's will—through His liberal bounty—condescends to accept the body of so humble a servant as worthy to receive His own inestimably precious Body.

O Lord Jesus, I adore Thee for the worth of Bread untold
Freely giv'n in Thy Communion, wonderful a thousandfold!
Giv'n today in loving bounty more than my poor heart can hold.
Make Thou of my soul an orchard quickened into fruitfulness;
Come, O come, life-giving Manna, making glad my wilderness;

Sweeter far than any sweetness tongue can taste, or words express!

JOHN MAUBERN, 1494;
TRANSLATED BY J.M.C. CRUM, 1932

FOR REFLECTION

"Good Lord, give me grace to long for Your holy sacraments, and especially to rejoice in the presence of Your truly blessed Body, sweet Savior Christ, in the holy sacrament of the altar, and to thank you duly for Your gracious visitation through it; and at that high memorial, may I have grace to remember and consider Your most bitter passion with tender compassion."

EVENING READING

Such is the wonderful bounty of almighty God, that He not only condescends, but He also delights to be with men, if they prepare to receive Him with honest and clean souls. For this reason he says: "My delight and pleasure is to be with the sons of men" [Prv 8:31]. And how can we doubt that God delights to be with the sons of men when the Son of God, who was truly the almighty God Himself, desired not only to become the Son of Man (that is, the son of Adam, the first man), but went even further to suffer in His innocent manhood His painful passion for the redemption and restitution of man?

Great Peril in the Eucharist

That is why many of you are weak and ill, and some have died.
But if we judged ourselves truly, we should not be judged.

1 CORINTHIANS 11:30-31

MORNING READING

Those who with outrageous wickedness intend to commit mortal sin even while they presume to receive the blessed Body of the Lord deserve to have the devil (with God's permission) enter their breasts so that they never again have the grace to cast him out. Instead, as a man with bridle and spurs rides and rules a horse, making him go whichever way he wants to guide him, so does the devil by his inward temptations govern and guide such a man, bridling him from all good and spurring him into all evil, till he drives him into a final mischief. For this is what the devil did to the false traitor Judas, who sinfully received that holy Body—the same man whom the devil rode in this way in order to pursue the traitorous death of the very same blessed Body of his most loving Master.

Thy table I approach; dear Savior, hear my prayer;
Oh, let no unrepented sin prove hurtful to me there!
Lo, I confess my sins and mourn their wretched bands;
A contrite heart is sure to find forgiveness at Thy hands.

GERHARD W. MOLANUS, 1673;
TRANSLATED BY MATTHIAS LOY, 1880

FOR REFLECTION

"Our most dear Savior Christ, who after completing Your own paschal sacrifice has instituted the new sacrament of Your own blessed Body and Blood as a memorial of Your bitter passion, give us such true faith in it and such fervent devotion to it that our souls may receive from it fruitful, spiritual food."

EVENING READING

If we presume irreverently to receive His precious, pure Pearl, the blessed Body of our Savior Himself, contained in the sacramental sign of bread, we will be like a herd of swine rooting in the dirt and wallowing in the mire. We will be treading it under the filthy feet of our foul inclinations, esteeming them more than we do the Sacrament, intending to walk and waddle in the puddle of foul, filthy sin. Thus a legion of demons may get permission from Christ to enter into us as they got his permission to enter into the hogs of Genezareth [see Mt 8:28-32]. And just as those devils drove the pigs on and never stopped until they drowned them in the sea, so might they drive us on and not fail to drown us in the deep sea of everlasting sorrow—unless God in His great mercy should restrain them and give us grace to repent.

God's Presence Remains With Us

He who eats my flesh and drinks my blood abides in me, and I in him.

JOHN 6:56

MORNING READING

Now when we have received our Lord and have Him in our body, let us not then leave Him alone as we get involved in other things, forgetting to look to Him anymore. For anyone who would serve a guest in such a way would have little sense! Instead, let all our concern be focused on Him. Let us by devout prayer talk to Him, by devout meditation talk with Him. Let us say with the prophet: "I will hear what our Lord will speak within me" [Ps 85:8]. For surely, if we set aside all other things and attend to Him, He will not fail to inspire us, to speak to us such things within us that will lead to the great spiritual comfort and profit of our soul.

Would that I could keep Thee always in mine inmost heart to be;
Thou and only Thou suggesting every thought and wish in me;
All my soul with singing offered for a sacrifice to Thee.

JOHN MAUBERN, 1494;
TRANSLATED BY J.M.C. CRUM, 1932

FOR REFLECTION
"Give me, good Lord, a longing to be with You."

EVENING READING
And therefore let us with Martha make sure that all our outward busyness may pertain to Him, in providing cheer for Him and to His company for His sake—namely, the poor. For whatever is done for every one of these, He considers it to be done not only for one of His disciples, but also for Himself. For He Himself said: "What you have done for one of the least of these my brethren, you have done for Me" [Mt 25:40]. And let us with Mary also sit in devout meditation and listen well to what our Savior, being now our Guest, will inwardly say to us.

The Eucharist, Source of Prayer and Good Works

As the living Father sent me, and I live because of the Father, so he who eats me will live because of me. This is the bread which came down from heaven.

JOHN 6:57-58a

MORNING READING

Having received the Blessed Sacrament, we have a special time of prayer. For He who made us, He who redeemed us, He whom we have offended, He who will judge us, He who will either damn us or save us, has because of His great goodness become our guest, and is personally present within us—and He has done that for no other purpose but to be sought for pardon so that He can save us. Let us not lose this time, therefore, nor allow this occasion to slip by, for we can hardly tell whether we shall ever get in to church again or not. Let us endeavor to keep Him always, and let us say with His two disciples who were going to the town of Emmaus, "Stay with us, good Lord" [Lk 24:29]. Then we shall be sure that He will not leave us, unless we ungratefully send Him away from us by our sin.

> *Ah, Lord Jesus, go not from me; stay, ah, stay with me, my Lord;*
> *Make me shrink from whatsoever will not with Thy name accord;*
> *Act through me in every action, speak through me in every word.*

JOHN MAUBERN, 1494;
TRANSLATED BY J.M.C. CRUM, 1932

FOR REFLECTION

"The things, good Lord, that I pray for, give me the grace to labor for."

EVENING READING

Let us receive Him in the Eucharist as He was received by the good tax collector Zacchacus—who, when he longed to see Christ, climbed up a tree because he was short in stature. Our Lord, seeing his devotion, called to him and said: "Zacchaeus, come down and come along, for this day I must stay with you" [Lk 19:5]. And he hurried to come down, and very gladly received Christ into his house. But he did not receive Him with only a fickle joy and soon-fading affection. Instead, so that it might be clear that he received Him with a sure, earnest and virtuous mind, he proved it by his virtuous works, making restitution to all those he had wronged. With such eagerness, such quickness of spirit, such gladness, such spiritual rejoicing as this man displayed when he received our Lord into his house, may our Lord give us the grace to receive His blessed Body and Blood, His holy Soul, and His almighty Godhead too into our bodies and into our souls. May the fruit of our good works bear witness to our conscience that we receive Him worthily and with the kind of full faith, with a firm purpose to live rightly, that we are obliged to have.

"His Glorious Presence…"

APPROACHING GOD IN PRAYER

Steadfast Prayer

Continue steadfastly in prayer, being watchful in it with thanksgiving.

COLOSSIANS 4:2

MORNING READING

In these words Christ commands us to be steadfast in prayer, and we are told that prayer is not only useful but also quite necessary. Why? Because without it, the weakness of the flesh holds us back until our minds, no matter how willing they may be to do good, are swept back into the evils of temptation. For who had a spirit more willing than Peter? And yet he had great need of God's protection against the flesh, which is clear enough from this single fact: When sleep kept him from praying and asking for God's help, he gave an opening to the devil, who soon afterward used the weakness of Peter's flesh to dull the eagerness of his spirit and pressed him to perjure himself by denying Christ.

My soul be on thy guard; ten thousand foes arise;
The hosts of sin are pressing hard to draw thee from the skies.
O watch, and fight, and pray; the battle ne'er give o'er;
Renew it boldly every day, and help divine implore.

LOWELL MASON, 1792–1872

FOR REFLECTION

"For the devil never runs upon a man to seize him with his claws until he sees him on the ground, already having fallen by his own will." Give me grace to stand, Father!

EVENING READING

Now if such things happened to the apostles, who were like thriving green branches—if even they fell into temptation when they allowed sleep to interrupt their prayers—what will become of us, who are like sapless twigs by comparison? What will we do when we are suddenly faced by danger—and when, I ask you, are we not in danger, since our enemy the devil continually prowls like a roaring lion, searching everywhere for someone who is ready to fall because of the weakness of the flesh, ready to pounce upon such a man and devour him? [see 1 Pt 5:8]. In such great peril, what will happen to us if we fail to follow Christ's counsel to be constant in wakefulness and prayer?

DAY 16
Pray Against Temptation

Watch and pray that you may not enter into temptation.

MATTHEW 26:41

MORNING READING

In the garden Christ tells us to stay awake, not to play cards and dice, not to get mixed up with rowdy parties and drunken brawls, not to find wine and women, but to pray. He tells us to pray not occasionally, but continually. "Pray," He says, "unceasingly" [see 1 Thes 5:17]. He tells us to pray not only during the day—for it is hardly necessary to tell anyone to stay awake during the day—but rather He exhorts us to devote to fervent prayer a large portion of that very time which most of us usually devote wholly to sleep. How ashamed we should be of our miserable failings when we recognize the immense guilt we incur by saying no more than a short prayer or two, perhaps, during the day—and saying those even as we doze and yawn.

Christian! Dost thou see them on the holy ground,
How the powers of darkness rage thy steps around?
Christian! Up and smite them, counting gain but loss,
In the strength that cometh by the holy cross.
Christian! Dost thou feel them, how they work within,
Striving, tempting, luring, goading into sin?
Christian! Never tremble; never be downcast;
Gird thee for the battle: Watch, and pray, and fast!

ANDREW OF CRETE, 660–732;
TRANSLATED BY JOHN MASON NEALE, 1818–66

FOR REFLECTION

"Almighty God, assist me with Your gracious help, so that I will never pay attention with the ears of my heart to the subtle suggestions of the serpent, but that my reason may instead resist them, and master my sensuality, and keep me from them."

EVENING READING

Our Savior tells us in the garden to pray, not that we may be wealthy, not that we may enjoy abundant pleasures, not that something evil may befall our enemies, not that we may receive honors in this world, but rather that we may not enter into temptation. In fact, He wishes us to understand that all those worldly goods are either harmful, or else, by comparison with that one great benefit, insignificant. So in His wisdom He placed this one petition at the end of the prayer He had previously taught His disciples, as if to serve as a summary of all the rest: "And lead us not into temptation, but deliver us from evil" [Mt 6:13].

Christ's Example of Thanksgiving and Prayer

In these days he went out into the hills to pray; and all night he continued in prayer to God.

LUKE 6:12

MORNING READING

"When Jesus had said these things, they sang the hymn and went out to the Mount of Olives" [Mt 26:30]. Although He had spoken at length about holiness during the supper with His apostles, still He finished His discourses with a hymn when it was time to leave. Alas, how different we are from Christ, even though we call ourselves Christians: Our mealtime conversation is without meaning or consequence (and even for that kind of negligence Christ warned us that we will have to give an account). Worse yet, often our table conversation is also injurious. Then at last, when we are swollen with food and drink, we leave the table without giving thanks to God for bestowing such a feast on us, with hardly a thought for the gratitude we owe Him. At most, we think it sufficient to say two or three words, and even those we only mutter for the sake of ritual, mumbling as we yawn.

Go to dark Gethsemane, ye that feel the tempter's power;
Your Redeemer's conflict see; watch with Him one bitter hour;
Turn not from His griefs away: learn of Jesus Christ to pray.
JAMES MONTGOMERY, 1771–1854

FOR REFLECTION

"Take from me, good Lord, this lukewarm—or rather cold-hearted—way of meditation, and this dullness in praying to You."

EVENING READING

"Judas, who betrayed Him, also knew the place, because Jesus frequently went there with His disciples" [Jn 18:2]. Once again the evangelists take the opportunity to note the betrayer in order to emphasize for us, and to recommend to us by their emphasis, Christ's holy habit of going together with His disciples to that place for prayer. Now where are those who think they are men of spiritual stature, who are proud of themselves as if they had done something wonderful, when occasionally, on the vigil of a special feast, they either continue their prayers a bit longer into the night or perhaps get up earlier for their morning prayers? Our Savior Christ had the habit of spending entire nights without sleep in order to pray. How I wish that those of us whose laziness keeps us from imitating the great example of our Savior might at least be willing to recall His all-night vigils whenever we turn over in our beds, half asleep—so that we might then, during the brief spell before we fall asleep again, give Him thanks, and condemn our laziness, and pray for additional grace. Surely if we make it a habit to do even the least little good, I am certain that God will soon send us forth a long way on the path of virtue.

Wandering Thoughts in Prayer

The Lord knows the thoughts of men, and that they are vain.
PSALM 94:11 NAB

MORNING READING

If only sometimes, just after we finish praying, we would try hard to review the time we have spent in prayer! What foolishness will we find there? What absurdity, or at times even filthiness, will we see? Indeed, we will be astonished that it was even possible for our minds to dissipate themselves in such a brief time among so many places so far apart from one another, among so many different affairs—such varied, such manifold, such idle pursuits! For if someone, simply as an experiment, should try with determination to make his mind touch on as many and as diverse objects as possible, I hardly think that in so short a time he could run through such diverse and numerous topics as the mind, unrestrained, wanders through while the mouth negligently mutters through the most common prayers.

Behold us, Lord, a little space from daily tasks set free,
And met within Thy holy place to rest awhile with Thee.
Around us rolls the ceaseless tide of business, toil and care,
And scarcely can we turn aside for one brief hour of prayer.
JOHN ELLERTON, 1826–93

FOR REFLECTION

"Give me, good Lord, a humble, lowly, quiet, peaceable, patient, charitable, kind, tender, and merciful mind, so that all my works, and all my words, and all my thoughts may have a taste of Your blessed Holy Spirit."

EVENING READING

If anyone should wonder or have any doubts about what the mind does when dreams take over our consciousness as we sleep, I find no comparison more apt than this: I think the mind is occupied as we sleep in precisely the same way as are the minds of those who are awake (if those who pray in this way can be said to be awake) but whose thoughts wildly roam as they pray They frantically flit about in a crowd of absurd fantasies—though with this one difference from the dreamer who sleeps: Some of the waking dreamer's strange visions, which his mind embraces in its wandering while his tongue rattles through his prayers as if they were only sound without sense—some of these strange sights, I say, are such lewd, abominable monsters that if they had been seen during sleep, certainly no one, no matter how shameless, would dare to recount such insane dreams after he woke up, not even in the company of stable boys.

DAY 19
Inattention in Prayer

O Lord ... you understand my thoughts from afar.... Where can I go from Your Spirit? from your presence where can I flee?

PSALM 139:1, 2, 7 NAB

MORNING READING

I simply cannot imagine how such distracted thoughts can enter into the minds of men as they pray—that is, as they speak to God—unless it happens through weakness of faith. Our minds do not go wandering while we address an earthly prince about some important matter or even while we speak to one of his ministers who might hold a position of some influence with his master. So surely it could never happen that our minds should stray even a little while we pray to God—surely not, that is, if we believed with a strong, lively faith that we are truly in the presence of God.

'Mid all the traffic of the ways—turmoils without, within,
Make in my heart a quiet place, and come and dwell therein.
A little shrine of quietness, all sacred to Thyself,
Where Thou shalt all my soul possess, and I may find myself.

JOHN OXENHAM, 1852–1941

FOR REFLECTION

"Give me, good Lord, warmth, delight, and liveliness as I think of You."

EVENING READING

Not only does God listen to our words and watch our countenance and bodily posture as outward signs and indicators of our interior state of mind; He also pierces into the most secret and inner recesses of our hearts with a penetrating vision. He illuminates everything with the light of His immeasurable majesty. So we could not possibly let our minds wander in prayer if we truly believed that God is present—the same God in whose glorious presence all the rulers of the world in all their glory must admit (unless they are deranged) that they are merely mites and earth-wallowing worms.

DAY 20
Respecting God's Presence

For we must all appear before the judgment seat of Christ, so that each one may receive good or evil, according to what he has done in the body.

2 CORINTHIANS 5:10

MORNING READING

Just imagine that you have committed a crime of high treason against some earthly prince or someone else who has your life in his hands. Suppose that he is so merciful that he is ready to temper his wrath because of your repentance and humble supplication, and to commute the death sentence into a monetary fine or even to suspend it completely if you convince him of your great shame and sorrow. Now, when you stand in the presence of the prince, try speaking to him carelessly, casually, without the least concern. While he sits still and gives you his attention, strut around here and there as you present your plea.... In short, conduct yourself in such a way that the prince can clearly see from your countenance, your voice, your gestures, and the entire posture of your body that while you are addressing him, you are actually thinking about something else. Tell me now: What possible success could you hope for from a plea like that?

Let all mortal flesh keep silence, and with fear and trembling stand;
Ponder nothing earthly-minded, for with blessing in His hand
Christ our God to earth descendeth, our full homage to demand.

FROM THE LITURGY OF SAINT JAMES;
TRANSLATED BY GERARD MOULTRIE, 1829–85

FOR REFLECTION

"A reverent attitude of the body, though it takes its origin and character from the soul, increases by a kind of reflex the soul's own reverence and devotion toward God." Lord, when I pray does my body reflect the reverence You deserve?

EVENING READING

Certainly we would think it truly insane to defend ourselves in such a disrespectful way before an earthly prince against a charge that threatens us with the death penalty. And yet such a prince, once he had destroyed our bodies, could do nothing more to us. So do we think it reasonable, when we have been caught committing an entire series of far more serious crimes, to act with such contempt as we beg pardon from the King of all kings, God Himself—who, when He has destroyed our bodies, has the power to send both body and soul together to hell [see Lk 12:4]?

Even so, I would not want anyone to understand what I have said to mean that I forbid anyone to pray while walking or sitting or even lying down. In fact, I wish that, whatever our bodies may be doing, we would at the same time continually lift up our minds to God, which is the most acceptable form of prayer. For no matter which way we may turn our steps, as long as our minds are turned to God, we clearly are not turned away from Him who is present everywhere. Yet I would insist that, besides the prayers we may say through the day while walking, we also should occasionally say some prayers for which we have prepared our minds more thoughtfully, for which we have disposed our bodies more reverently, than we would if we were about to approach all the rulers in the whole world seated together in one place.

DAY 21
Praying at Night

Rise and pray that you may not enter into temptation.

LUKE 22:46

MORNING READING

The apostles waiting for Christ in the garden have just learned twice by experience that when they remain sitting, they only grow drowsy, and sleep gradually slips up on them. So He teaches them an instant cure for that sluggish sickness of sleepiness—namely, to get up. Since this kind of remedy was given by our Savior Himself, I earnestly wish that we would occasionally be willing to try it out in the middle of the night. For here we would find not only that "well begun is half done," but also that once begun is all done. For when we are fighting off sleep, the first battle is always the most fierce.

Softly now the light of day fades upon our sight away;
Free from care, from labor free, Lord, we would commune
*   with Thee.*
Thou, whose all-pervading eye naught escapes without, within,
Pardon each infirmity, open fault and secret sin.

GEORGE W. DOANE, 1799–1859

FOR REFLECTION

"If we try to escape sadness by seeking our consolation in sleep, we will fail to find what we are seeking, for we will lose in sleep the consolation we might have received from God if we had stayed awake and prayed." Teach me, Jesus, to watch and pray in the night.

EVENING READING

For this reason, when we are tempted to sleep instead of pray, we should not try to overcome the temptation by a prolonged struggle. Instead we should break with one blow the embrace of the enticing arms with which sleep enfolds us and pulls us down, and we should run away from it all of a sudden. Then, once we have thrown off idle sleep, the very image of death, life with all its enthusiasm will return. Then, if we give ourselves to meditation and prayer, the soul, collected in that dark silence of the night, will discover that it is much more open to divine consolation than it is during the daytime, when the noise of business all around distracts the eyes, the ears, and the mind, and dissipates our energy in countless activities that are as meaningless as they are varied.

But Christ have mercy! How is it that even though thoughts about some trivial, worldly matter may at times wake us and keep us awake for a long time, hardly letting us go back to sleep at all, on the other hand prayer somehow fails to keep us awake! In spite of the great loss of spiritual benefits, in spite of the many traps set for us by our mortal enemy, in spite of the peril of being utterly ruined, we do not wake up to pray, but lie instead in a drugged sleep, enjoying the dreams brought on by the sleeping potions we have taken.

The Help of the Angels and Saints

And there appeared to him an angel from heaven, strengthening him.

LUKE 22:43

MORNING READING

Do you realize how severe Christ's mental anguish must have been, that an angel should come from heaven to strengthen Him? But when I think about these words, I cannot help wondering how harmful is the nonsense of those who argue that it is useless for anyone to seek the intercession of any angel or departed saint. They claim that this is so because we can confidently address our prayers to God Himself, not only because He alone is more present to us than all the angels and all the saints together, but also because He has the power to grant us more, and a greater desire to do so, than any of the saints in heaven, of whatever kind. With trivial and groundless arguments such as these, they display their envy and displeasure at the glory of the saints. But the saints themselves are in turn equally displeased with such men, who try to undermine the loving honor we pay to the saints and to the saving help they give us.

Why shouldn't these shameless men who argue this way follow the same logic and contend that the angel's labor to console our Savior Christ was totally pointless and unnecessary? For what angel among all the heavenly hosts was as powerful as Christ Himself or as near to Him as God, since He Himself was God?

Jesus, Brightness of the Father, Life and Strength of all who live,
For creating guardian angels, glory to Thy name we give.
Blessed Lord, by their protection shelter us from harm this day,
Keep us pure in flesh and spirit, save us from the foe, we pray.

RHABANUS MAURUS, 856;
TRANSLATED BY EDWARD CASWALL, 1814–78

FOR REFLECTION

"O glorious blessed Trinity, may I through the merits of Christ's bitter passion be a partner in Your blessedness with those holy spirits who stood faithful to You and, now confirmed by Your grace, will stand forever in glory."

EVENING READING

Those in the Catholic Church, whom some rebuke for praying to saints and going on pilgrimages, do not seek any saint as their savior. Instead, they seek saints as those whom their Savior loves, and whose intercession and prayer for the seeker He will be content to hear. For His own sake, He would have those He loves honored. And when they are thus honored for His sake, then the honor that is given them for His sake overflows especially to Himself. As Christ Himself said, whoever hears them hears Him, and whoever despises them despises Him, and in the same way whoever glorifies them for His sake glorifies Him.

Why Ask the Saints to Pray?

To this end we always pray for you, that our God may make you worthy of his call, and may fulfil every good resolve and work of faith by his power, so that the name of our Lord Jesus may be glorified in you, and you in Him, according to the grace of our God and the Lord Jesus Christ.

2 THESSALONIANS 1:11-12

MORNING READING

You say you see no reason why we should pray to the saints since God can hear us and help us just as well, and will do so gladly, as any saint in heaven. Well, then, what need, I ask, do you have to ask any physician to help your fever, or to ask and pay any surgeon to heal your sore leg? For God can both hear you and help you as well as the best of doctors. He loves you more than they do, and He can help you sooner. Besides—his poultices are cheaper, and He will give you more for your words alone than they will for your money!

But it is His pleasure, you say, that I should be helped my means of those who are His instruments—in fact, he Himself works through them, since He is the One who has given the doctors' remedies their healing nature.

In the same way, I say, it has pleased God that we should ask assistance from His holy saints, and pray to them for help. Nor does that make them equal to God Himself, whether they help us by His will and power or He helps us because of their intercession.

We cannot think of them as dead who walk with us no more
Along the path of life we tread; they have but gone before.
And still their silent ministries within our hearts have place,
As when on earth they walked with us and met us face to face.
Ours are they by an ownership nor time nor death can free;
For God hath given to love to keep its own eternally.

FREDERICK L. HOSMER, 1840–1929

FOR REFLECTION

"If Saint Paul exhorts us to pray for one another, and we gladly think it right to ask every poor man to pray for us, should we think it evil to ask the holy saints in heaven to do the same?" Saints of God, help us with your intercession.

EVENING READING

Though God is, as reason teaches us, above all and has no equal, He does not forbid us to ask others besides Himself for help. And though the Father has given all judgment to the Son [see Jn 5:22], yet He delights to have His holy saints as partners in that honor, and to be seated at His side on the day of judgment [see 1 Cor 6:2-3]. Was Elisha made equal to God because the widow asked him to revive her dead son? Were the apostles equal to Christ because they were asked for help after His death—and even during His life on earth? Do you actually think, then, that if He were happy to give men occasion to petition these saints while they were with Him on earth, He will be angry if we pay them the same honor when they are with Him in heaven?

DAY 24
How the Saints Hear Us

These all died in faith.... Therefore God is not ashamed to be
called their God, for he has prepared for them a city.... Since
we are surrounded by so great a cloud of witnesses, let us also
lay aside every weight, and sin which clings so closely, and let us
run with perseverance the race that is set before us, looking to
Jesus the pioneer and perfecter of our faith.

HEBREWS 11:13, 16; 12:1-2

MORNING READING

You may marvel and think it hard to believe that the saints hear
us. Yet seeing that the things we ask them for, we obtain, I
marvel even more how men can doubt whether or not their
prayers are heard.

The wonder is how they can see and hear in various places at
once. Think of it this way: If there were creatures who could
only feel, and could not see or hear, they too would wonder
how it could be possible for us to do such things. Or if they
didn't wonder about the matter because they had never even
heard of sights and sounds, they would be far from even
conceiving in their minds that it would be possible for
someone to have senses extending farther than they could feel.
And even though by our seeing and hearing, we prove that
such things are possible, yet even we ourselves don't
understand fully how our sense organs work.

Come, let us join our friends above who have obtained the
prize,
And on the eagle wings of love to joys celestial rise.
One family we dwell in Him, One Church, above, beneath,
Though now divided by the stream, the narrow stream of death.

One army of the living God, to His command we bow;
Part of His host have crossed the flood, and part are crossing
now.

CHARLES WESLEY, 1707–88

FOR REFLECTION

"Considering that when the saints lived in this world they were
at liberty to roam the earth, do you really think that in heaven
God would have them tied to a post?" Saints of God, thank
you for your intercession!

EVENING PRAYER

Now considering that we can with our fleshly eyes, while still in
this earthly body, see and hear things that are at some distance
from us, and from one another, should we marvel so much
that the blessed angels and holy souls, being purely spiritual
substances and unhindered by all the burden of flesh and
bones, can do the same? or that they can far surpass and excel
our natural powers—just as the living soul itself surpasses the
mortal body? We find that the saints do indeed help us; why
then refuse to believe that they hear us unless we understand
the means by which they do it? What does it matter whether
they see and hear us by coming to us here on earth, or by our
voice reaching up to them in heaven? whether God hears and
sees everything, and then shows it to them, or whether they
behold it all in Him just as someone reads something in a
book? or whether God by some other way tells it to them? Will
we refuse to believe that it happens unless we know how? That
would be about as wise as refusing to believe that you can see
simply because you don't understand how your eyes work!

"Diligent Labor..."

THE VIRTUOUS LIFE

DAY 25
Loving God First

You shall love the Lord your God with all your heart, and with all your soul, and with all your mind, and with all your strength.

MARK 12:30

MORNING READING

Let every man, therefore, in time learn, as we should, to love God above all other things, and to love all other things for His sake. And whatever love is not based on that purpose—namely, the pleasure of God—it is a very vain and an unfruitful love. And whatever love we bear to any creature in such a way that we love God the less, that love is a loathsome love and hinders us from heaven. Love no child of your own so tenderly that you could not be content to sacrifice him to God as Abraham was ready to do with Isaac, if God were to command you to do so. And since we know that God would never do that, offer your child otherwise to God's service.

Jesus, Thy boundless love to me no thought can reach, no tongue declare;
O knit my thankful heart to Thee and reign without a rival there!
Thine wholly, Thine alone I'd live
Myself to Thee entirely give.

PAUL GERHARDT, 1607–76;
TRANSLATED BY JOHN WESLEY, 1703–91

FOR REFLECTION

"Give me, good Lord, such a love for You that I will love nothing in a way that displeases You, and I will love everything for Your sake."

EVENING READING

For if our love for something causes us to break God's commandment, then we love it better than we love God—and that is a love both deadly and damnable. Now, since our Lord has so loved us enough to make possible our salvation, let us diligently call for His grace, so that we might not be found ungrateful in return for His great love. O my sweet Savior Christ, who, because of Your undeserved love for mankind, would so kindly suffer the painful death of the cross, don't allow me to be cold or lukewarm in the love I return to You!

No Virtue Without Obedience

Peter said to [Jesus], "You shall never wash my feet."

JOHN 13:8a

MORNING READING

Jesus came to Saint Peter to wash his feet. But Saint Peter had imprinted deeply in his breast the marvelous, high majesty of the person of Christ—His being the very Son of God, and equal to His almighty Father and His Holy Spirit, and one God with Them, and therefore being infinitely more in dignity above the apostle than the heaven is in distance above the earth. So Saint Peter, despite His Savior's command, could not find it in his heart to allow the Lord to perform for him such a simple, humble service. But our Lord spoke sharply to him and said: "Unless I wash you, you will have no part in me" [Jn 13:8]. In this way our Lord showed him that no virtue could ever be of benefit without a humble obedience to God. In fact, attempts to be virtuous that are joined to disobedience to the will of God, no matter how good they may appear, will actually work for our damnation.

Have Thine own way, Lord! Have Thine own way!
Thou art the Potter; I am the clay.
Mold me and make me after Thy will,
while I am waiting, yielded and still.
Have Thine own way, Lord! Have Thine own way!
Hold o'er my being absolute sway!
Fill with Thy Spirit, till all shall see
Christ only, always, living in me!

ADELAIDE A. POLLARD, 1862–1904

FOR REFLECTION

"Lord, give me grace in everything to conform my will to Yours, so that I may truly say: 'Thy will be done, on earth as it is in heaven.'"

EVENING READING

Holy teachers of the Church have commented on this biblical passage, in which Saint Peter, out of a sense of reverence, refuses to receive what our Lord wants to do for him. They have noted that no man may legitimately do what God has forbidden nor leave undone what God has commanded by claiming that he does so according to his own private understanding of what reverence or devotion requires. For this would be an imprudent devotion, and an irreverent reverence, and not at all a proper humility. It is instead only an unrecognized pride to stand stubbornly against God's will and to disobey His pleasure. For as the Scripture says: "Better is obedience than sacrifice" [1 Sm 15:22].

Knowledge Versus Obedience

If you know these things, blessed are you if you do them.

JOHN 13:17

MORNING READING

In these words, spoken after He had washed His disciples' feet, our Savior clearly declares that the bliss of heaven will not be attained by knowing about virtue, but rather by becoming virtuous. No man can come to the town of Canterbury simply by knowing the way there if he insists on sitting at home; in the same way, merely knowing the way to heaven can never take us there unless we are willing to walk in that way. And therefore our Lord says by the mouth of the prophet: "Blessed are those whose way is blameless, who walk in the law of the Lord ... those who do no wrong, but walk in His ways" [Ps 119:1, 3].

Take my life and let it be consecrated, Lord, to Thee.
Take my moments and my days; let them flow in ceaseless praise.
Take my hands and let them move at the impulse of Thy love.
Take my feet and let them be swift and beautiful for Thee.
Take my will and make it Thine; it shall be no longer mine.

FRANCES R. HAVERGAL, 1836-79

FOR REFLECTION

"Even though we well know and believe what is good, the world, and the frailty of our flesh, and the enticement of our spiritual enemies, makes us willingly and knowingly walk in what is evil." Lord, does my knowledge of Your will lead me to obedience?

EVENING READING

And our Savior says with His own mouth that knowledge without work not only profits a man nothing, but also causes an increase of his punishment compared to what his punishment would be if, without his willful ignorance, his knowledge had been much less. For thus says our Lord: "The servant who does not know the will of his master and does not do it will receive only a few lashes. But the servant who knows his master's will and does not do it will receive many lashes" [Lk 12:47-48]. And therefore with this necessary, fruitful doctrine our Lord summed it all up: "If you know these things, and do them indeed, then shall you be blessed; but if you only know them and neglect to do them, you will be worse off."

Faith, Works, and Grace

For as the body apart from the spirit is dead, so faith apart from works is dead.

JAMES 2:26

MORNING READING

The Church believes that without grace man's will is incapable of performing good deeds; but like the light of the sun, grace is available to all. Evil men neglect it when it is offered to them, while good men embrace it. And both do what they do by their own free will. Thus a man who is saved is saved by grace, and yet his free will is not without its role.

I do not see anything except by the light; yet I help the light to some extent when I open my eyes and focus them. If a man lowers a rope into a well and pulls someone out who could not escape by himself, wouldn't it be true that the man in the well did not climb out by his own power? And yet he still contributed something of his own to the process by hanging on to the rope and not letting it get away. The freedom of the will is like that: It can do nothing without grace. But when the divine goodness grants grace generously, the free will of a good man holds fast to it and cooperates with it properly. But the free will of an evil man does not accept grace; it wears itself out in malice.

When we walk with the Lord in the light of His Word
What a glory He sheds on our way!
While we do His good will, He abides with us still,
And with all who will trust and obey.

JOHN H. SAMMIS, 1846–1919

FOR REFLECTION

"For grace is the light by which men see the way to walk out of sin; and grace is the staff without whose help no man is able to rise out of sin." Lord, I need Your grace!

EVENING READING

A man who admits that he cannot perform good works without grace does not struggle against grace by trying to do good works. Rather, he does not, like the Pharisee, rely on works, for he knows they are worthless without faith and can merit no reward except through God's generosity alone. Those who are clearly opposed to grace and utterly deny Christ are actually the ones who exalt grace and trust in the faith of Christ so that they can make men lukewarm in doing good. They utterly deny that good works have any goodness or merit in them at all, while we condemn only the sinful reliance on works. When men are slow to do good, they fast lose both faith and grace. For we find far more men who would rather believe well than do well.

The Good Example of a Good Example

*For I have given you an example, that you also should do as I
have done to you.*

JOHN 13:15

MORNING READING

Would to God that all the church officials, and all the parish
pastors, and all the preachers—yes, and fathers and mothers,
and all masters of households too—would follow the example
given here of our Savior, which is to provide others with a
good example themselves. There are many who can be well
content only to preach: some to show their knowledge and
some to show their authority. But would to God they would
act in the manner that our Savior acted, namely, to first do
themselves the things they bid other men do. The Scripture
says of our Savior, "Jesus began to do and to teach" [Acts 1:1];
He not only taught men to do this or that, but He also gave
them an example and did the thing first Himself.

Let the beauty of Jesus be seen in me,
All His wonderful passion and purity;
O Thou Spirit divine, all my nature refine,
Till the beauty of Jesus be seen in me.

ALBERT ORSBORN

FOR REFLECTION

"Whoever bids other folks to do right, but gives an evil example by acting the opposite way, is like a foolish weaver who weaves quickly with one hand and unravels the cloth just as quickly with the other." What kind of example do I set, Lord?

EVENING READING

To stir us to fast, Jesus not only taught us how we should do it, but also became our example by fasting forty days Himself. To stir us to stay awake and pray, He not only taught us by word, but He also used to go out at night to the Mount of Olivet, where He stayed awake and prayed through the night—a habit that allowed the traitor Judas to know where to find Him. He not only taught us by word to place no value on the royalty of the world; by His birth in poverty, and the poverty of the entire course of His life, He gave us the example Himself. To stir us to patience in suffering tribulation, He not only taught us and exhorted us by word; He gave us the example of His own cross, His own Passion, and His own painful death.

Focusing on Others' Faults

Why do you see the speck that is in your brother's eye, but do not notice the log that is in your own eye? Or how can you say to your brother, "Let me take the speck out of your eye," when there is the log in your own eye? You hypocrite, first take the log out of your own eye, and then you will see clearly to take the speck out of your brother's eye.

MATTHEW 7:3-5

MORNING READING

We look more upon the vices of others than on our own. It is just as Aesop once put it in a fable: Every man carries a double wallet over his shoulders. Into the one that hangs on his chest he puts the faults of other folks, which he carries around and examines often. But in the other he collects all his own faults, letting them swing behind his back where it never pleases him to look—though others that come after him like to look through all its contents. Would to God that we were all of the mind to think that no man is as bad as ourselves! For that would be the way to mend both them and ourselves. But as it is now, they blame us, and we blame them, though both sides are actually worthy of blame, and both are more ready to find others' faults than they are to correct their own.

God, be merciful to me; on Thy grace I rest my plea;
Plenteous in compassion Thou, blot out my transgressions now.
Wash me, make me pure within; cleanse, O cleanse me from
   my sin.
My transgressions I confess; grief and guilt my soul oppress;

*I have sinned against Thy grace, and provoked Thee to Thy
    face;*
I confess thy judgment just; speechless, I Thy mercy trust.
THE PSALTER, 1912; FROM PSALM 51

FOR REFLECTION

"We would all much better mend our ways if we were as ready
to pray for one another as we are to offer one another reproach
and rebuke." Father, show me my faults as You see them.

EVENING READING

We are so studious in our efforts to reproach others that
neither good nor bad passes unreproved. If they are friendly,
we call them frivolous. If they keep to themselves, we call them
daydreamers. If they are sad, we call them solemn. If they are
merry, we call them crazy. If they are sociable, we call them
sinful. If they are holy, we call them hypocrites. If they keep
few servants we call them pinch-pennies. If they keep many we
call them pompous. If a wicked priest does a wicked deed, then
we say, "Look! See what an example the clergy sets for us"—as
if that one priest were the whole clergy. But then we forget to
look for what good men might be among the clergy, and what
good counsel they give us, and what a good example they
provide us.

We act like ravens and carrion crows who never bother with
any living flesh—but wherever we may find a dead dog in a
ditch, that's where we fly to stuff ourselves. In the same way,
when we see a good man, and hear or see a good thing, then
we take little heed. But when once we see an evil deed, then
we stop and stare; and all day long we gossip and feed
ourselves with the filthy delight of evil conversation.

Finishing the Work God Gives Us to Do

The time of my departure has come. I have fought the good fight, I have finished the race, I have kept the faith. Henceforth there is laid up for me the crown of righteousness, which the Lord, the righteous judge, will award to me on that Day.

2 TIMOTHY 4:6-8

MORNING READING

Our Savior knew when He would die yet He was diligent to do those things that He had to do before His death—even though He could have deferred His death until the time He chose, and in the meantime done everything at ease and leisure. But we are poor wretches who will die before we wish, and who cannot tell the time when, but may even die today. How urgent it is, then, that we make haste about those things that we must do, so that we may have nothing left undone when we are suddenly sent for and must go. For when death comes, the dreadful, mighty messenger of God, no king can command him, no authority can restrain him, no riches can hire him to wait past his appointed time even one moment of an hour. Therefore let us consider well in time what words we are bound to speak and what deeds we are bound to do, and let us say them and do them quickly. And let us leave unsaid and undone all superfluous things (and, much more, all damnable things), knowing well that we have no empty time allowed to us.

To serve the present age, my calling to fulfill,
O may it all my powers engage to do my Master's will!
Arm me with jealous care, as in Thy sight to live,
And oh, Thy servant, Lord, prepare a strict account to give!

CHARLES WESLEY, 1707–88

FOR REFLECTION

"God, give us all the grace to do all our duty in time so that we will not spend our time in vanities, or worse than vanities, while we are yet in health, or drive off the things of substance that we should be doing till we lie in our death bed—for otherwise, when that last hour comes, we shall have so many things to do at once, and everything will be so unready, that every finger shall be a thumb and we shall fumble in haste so clumsily that it may happen—unless You help us—that we will leave more than half undone."

EVENING READING

Let us then always make ourselves ready for death, with nothing left undone. May we by the help of His grace be able to say to ourselves and our friends every day, "I have done all my duty, all I have come into this world to do; for I shall some day—though I don't know how soon (perhaps even today)—be delivered by God to the cross of painful death." And if I die wicked, I will depart from death to the devil, as did the blasphemous thief who hung on his cross beside Christ. And if I die well, as I trust in God to do, I may with His mercy depart directly into paradise, as did the penitent thief who hung on His other side.

DAY 32
Weeding Out Ungodly Pleasures

It has happened to them according to the true proverb, The dog turns back to his own vomit, and the sow is washed only to wallow in the mire.

2 PETER 2:22

MORNING READING

Just as a sick man tastes no sweetness in sugar, and some women with child have such strange cravings that they had rather eat tar than molasses and pitch rather than marmalade, and some entire nations love tallow more than butter, and the people of Iceland don't like butter unless it has been aged in a barrel, in the same way we gross, carnal people have had our tastes infected by the sickness of sin and the filthy habit of fleshly lust. We find so great a liking in the vile and stinking enjoyment of fleshly delight that we never desire even once to prove what manner of sweetness that good and virtuous folk feel and perceive in spiritual pleasure. And this is the cause: We cannot perceive the one unless we shun the other.

> *God calling yet! Shall I not hear? Earth's pleasures shall I still hold dear?*
> *Shall life's swift-passing years all fly, and still my soul in slumber lie?*
> *God calling yet! And shall I give no heed, but still in bondage live?*
> *I wait, but He does not forsake; he calls me still—my heart, awake!*

GERHARD TERSTEEGEN, 1697–1769;
TRANSLATED BY JANE BORTHWICK, 1813–97

FOR REFLECTION

"Good virtuous folks feel more pleasure in the sorrow of their sins and the affliction of their penance than wretches feel in the fulfilling of their foul pleasure." Do I take pleasure in repentance, Father?

EVENING READING

Just as the ground that is all overgrown with nettles, briars, and other evil weeds can bring forth no grain until these are weeded out, so our soul can have no place for the good grain of spiritual pleasure, as long as it is overgrown with the barren weeds of carnal enjoyment. And for the pulling out of these weeds by the root, there is no more fitting tool than the remembrance of our final destiny—which, just as it pulls out the weeds of sensual gratification, cannot fail to plant in their places not only wholesome virtues, but also marvelous spiritual pleasure and gladness. These rise in every good soul from the love of God, and the hope of heaven, and the inward pleasure that the godly spirit takes in the diligent labor of good and virtuous business.

DAY 33

Perverting Good Things for Evil Purposes

[Judas] went up to [Jesus] at once, and said, "Master!" And he kissed Him.

MARK 14:45

MORNING READING

When Judas betrays Him, Christ reviles the blasphemous hypocrisy of the traitor: "With a kiss," He says, "do you betray the Son of Man?" Among all the circumstances surrounding an evil deed it is hard to find one more hateful to God than the perversion of the real nature of good things to make them into instruments of our malice. Thus lying is hateful to God because words, which He appointed to express the mind's meaning, are twisted to deceptive purposes. Within this category of evil, it is a grave offense against God to misuse the law to inflict the very injuries it was intended to prevent.

Who was the guilty? Who brought this upon Thee?
Alas, my treason, Jesus, hath undone Thee!
'Twas I, Lord Jesus, I it was denied Thee:
I crucified Thee!

JOHANN HEERMANN, 1585–1647;
TRANSLATED BY ROBERT BRIDGES, 1844–1930

FOR REFLECTION

"The devil's primary enterprise and proudest triumph consists in the bringing of a man to abuse that thing which is best in his own nature." What is it in me, Lord, that the devil is trying to abuse?

EVENING READING

And so Christ rebukes Judas sharply for this detestable type of sin, the perversion of what is good to an evil purpose: "Judas," He says, "do you betray the Son of Man with a kiss?" ... For whoever commits such an unfriendly deed while posing as a friend is a villain who multiplies his villainy. Was it not enough for you to betray this Son of Man without doing it with a kiss, thus turning the most sacred sign of charity into an instrument of betrayal? Certainly I am more favorably disposed toward this mob which attacks me with open force than toward you, Judas, who betray me to the attackers with a false kiss.

Hope for the Worst of Sinners

The steadfast love of the Lord never ceases, his mercies never come to an end; they are new every morning; great is thy faithfulness.

LAMENTATIONS 3:22-23

MORNING READING

There is no limit to the mercy of a gracious God. Even to Judas God gave many opportunities for repentance. He did not deny him His friendship. He did not strip him of the dignity of his apostleship. He did not even take from him their common purse, even though he was a thief. He allowed the traitor into the fellowship of His beloved disciples at the Last Supper. He condescended to stoop down before His betrayer, and with His sacred, innocent hands to wash Judas' filthy feet—a fitting symbol of his filthy mind. Moreover, with generosity beyond compare, Christ gave him to eat, in the form of bread, that very Body of His which the betrayer had already sold. And under the appearance of wine, He gave him that very Blood to drink which, even as he drank it, the traitor was wickedly plotting to tap and set flowing. At last when Judas, coming with his gang to seize Him, gave Him a kiss—a kiss that was actually the abominable token of his treachery—Christ received him calmly and gently.

There's a wideness in God's mercy like the wideness of the sea;
There's a kindness in His justice which is more than liberty.
There is welcome for the sinner, and more graces for the good;
There is mercy with the Savior; there is healing in His blood.

FREDERICK W. FABER, 1814—

FOR REFLECTION

"When we see anyone roaming far from the right path, let us hope that he will one day return to the road, and meanwhile let us pray humbly, without ceasing, that God will hold out to him opportunities to repent. Let us pray as well that with God's help he will eagerly seize those opportunities, and having seized them, will hold them fast." Father, grant Your mercy to those who have run far from You.

EVENING READING

Who wouldn't believe that any one of all Christ's kindnesses to Judas could have turned his treacherous mind, however calloused by crime, to a better way? Then too, consider the beginning of repentance Judas displayed: when he confessed that he had sinned, and gave back the silver pieces, and threw them away when they were refused, crying out that he was a traitor and admitting that he had betrayed innocent blood. I must believe that Christ prompted him to this point so that He might if possible save Judas from destruction—the very man who had so recently, so wickedly, betrayed Him to death. But instead, the traitor added despair to his treachery and perished.

Therefore, since God displayed His great mercy in so many ways even toward Judas, an apostle turned traitor, since He invited him so often to be forgiven and did not allow him to perish except through despair alone, surely there is no cause for anyone in this life to despair even of an imitator of Judas. Instead, according to that holy counsel of the apostle, "Pray for each other that you may be saved" [Jas 5:16].

"Dirt and Mire..."

THOSE DEADLY SINS

The Pride of Status and Beauty

He has shown strength with his arm, he has scattered the proud in the imagination of their hearts.

LUKE 1:51

MORNING READING

We should consider well this matter, and ponder well this fearful point: What horrible peril there is in the pestilent sin of pride! What abominable sin it is in the sight of God when any creature falls into being enamored of itself. If this continues, what inevitably follows is this: First the neglect of God, and then the contempt of God, and finally, through disobedience and rebellion, the utter forsaking of God.

God was so displeased with pride that He did not spare to drive down into hell the noble, high, excellent angels of heaven for the sake of their pride. So who in this wretched world could have a status so high that he would not have serious cause to tremble and quake in every joint of his body as soon as he feels a high, proud thought enter his heart? Remember the terrible threat of God in holy scripture: The mighty men shall mightily suffer torments [see Wis 6:6].

"Take up thy cross," the Savior said, "if thou wouldst My
disciple be;
Deny thyself, the world forsake, and humbly follow after Me."
Take up thy cross, nor heed the shame; nor let thy foolish pride
rebel;
Thy Lord for thee the cross endured to save thy soul from death
and hell.

CHARLES W. EVEREST, 1814–77

FOR REFLECTION

"O glorious blessed Trinity, whose justice has damned to perpetual pain many proud, rebellious angels ... for the sake of
Your tender mercy, plant in my heart such meekness that I may
by Your grace follow the promptings of my guardian angel,
and resist the proud suggestions of those spiteful spirits who
fell."

EVENING READING

If it is such a grievous thing, and so unfitting in the sight of
God, to see the sin of pride in the person of high estate—who
has many temptations to be inclined to such sin—how much
more abominable is such foolish pride in a low-class, prodigal
rascal whose purse is as penniless as any poor peddler, yet
whose heart is as uppity as many a mighty prince. And if it is
disgusting in the sight of God that a woman who is beautiful
indeed should allow pride in her beauty to lead to vainglory,
how delightful to the devil is that dainty damsel who stands
looking at herself and considers herself pretty—thinking herself
well admired for her broad forehead while the young man
looking at her focuses more on her crooked nose.

The Pride of Possessions

They trust in their wealth; the abundance of their riches is their boast. Yet in no way can a man redeem himself, or pay his own ransom to God.

PSALM 49:7-8 NAB

MORNING READING

If it is detestable for any creature to rise up in pride for the sake of status, beauty, strength, intellect, or learning—or anything else that by nature and grace are properly their own—how much more foolish corruption is there in that pride by which we worldly folks look up on high, and solemnly esteem ourselves, with a deep disdain for other, far better, men, only for the sake of quite vain, worldly trifles that are not properly our own! How proud we are of gold and silver, which are actually no part of ourselves, but rather are part of the earth—things that are by their nature no better than poor copper or tin, and much less useful than the poor metal that is used to make the ploughshare, and horseshoes, and horse nails.

I am coming to the cross; I am poor, and weak, and blind;
I am counting all but dross; I shall full salvation find.

WILLIAM MCDONALD, 1820–1901

FOR REFLECTION

"May Almighty God grant both you and me, and all mortal men everywhere, to count as nothing all the riches of this world, and all the glory of it."

EVENING READING

How proud many men are of those glistening precious stones, of which the very brightest, even if it costs many dollars, will never shine half so bright nor show half so much light as a poor halfpenny candle! How proud is many a man who looks down on his neighbor because the wool of his gown is finer! Yet as fine as it is, a poor sheep wore it on her back before it came upon his back, and all the while she wore it, no matter how fine her wool was, she was after all still only a sheep. And why should he now be better than she was simply by having that wool—wool that, even though it is now his, is still not so truly his as it was truly hers?

DAY 37

Our Possessions Are on Loan

What have you that you did not receive? If then you received it,
why do you boast as if it were not a gift?

1 CORINTHIANS 4:7b

MORNING READING

But now how many men are there who are proud of what is not really theirs at all? We are like someone who is proud of keeping another man's gate, or another man's horse, or another man's hound or hawk. We are like a bear-keeper who brags about the silver-buttoned belt of his uniform—who takes pride in keeping another man's bear! Isn't that how we talk about the things we consider to be ours and others' possessions? If we consider the matter rightly, I can see nothing that any man can well call his own. But just as men may call the one a fool who bears himself proudly because he struts about in a borrowed suit, so may all of us too be rightly called true fools if we take pride in anything that we have in this life. For nothing we have here is our own, not even our own bodies.

We give Thee but Thine own, whate'er the gift may be:
All that we have is Thine alone, a trust, O Lord, from Thee.
WILLIAM WALSHAM HOW, 1823–97

FOR REFLECTION

"We have borrowed everything from God, and we must return it to Him again, and send our helpless soul out naked—nor can any man tell how soon." What is it in my life, Lord, that I treat as if it were my own to keep?

EVENING READING

All that we ever have, we have received from God: riches, royalty, power, beauty, strength, learning, intellect, body, soul, and all. And almost all these things He has only lent us. For all these we must leave behind someday, except only our soul. Even that must we give back to God again also—or else we will keep it forever in hell with such sorrow that we would be better off losing it. And for the misuse of our souls and of our bodies with them, and of all the remains of those borrowed goods of which we are now so proud, we will give a full and strict accounting and face a heavy reckoning. Then many a thousand men, body and soul together, will burn in hell eternally for foolish pride over those borrowed goods which previously they had boasted about with such vainglory in the brief, transitory time so soon passed in this foolish, wretched world.

The Torment of Envy

Envy is the rottenness of the bones.

PROVERBS 14:30b, DOUAY-RHEIMS

MORNING READING

The sickness of envy is undoubtedly both a serious torment and a consuming disease. For surely envy is such a torment that all the tyrants in Sicily have never devised a worse torture. It drinks up the moisture of the body and consumes the good blood. It discolors the face, and defaces its beauty, disfiguring the appearance and leaving it all bony, lean, pale, and sickly. For that reason, a person busily engaged in envy needs no other image of death than his own face in a mirror. This vice is not only devilish, but also very foolish: For even though envy, whenever it has the power, does all the hurt it can, yet since the worse most commonly envies the better, and the weaker, the stronger, it happens most often that the envious person frets, fumes, and burns in his own heart, without the ability to hurt the one he envies. He is like the fire of the burning mountain of Etna, which only burns itself.

With forbidden pleasures would this vain world charm,
And its sordid treasures spread to work me harm.
Bring to my remembrance sad Gethsemane,
Or, in darker semblance, cross-crowned Calvary.

JAMES MONTGOMERY, 1771–1854

FOR REFLECTION

"Such is the wretched appetite of this cursed envy: ready to run into the fire, so that he may draw his neighbor with him!" Show me how to repent of my envy, Lord.

EVENING READING

I remember a certain fable of Aesop that expresses so fittingly the nature, the feeling, and the reward of two capital vices, namely envy and covetousness. Aesop, as I think you have heard, told how one of the pagan gods came down to earth and found two men together in the same place, one of them envious and the other covetous. He showed himself willing to give each of them a gift, but one of them had to request the gift for them both, and whatever he asked for himself, the other would have the same thing doubled. When this condition was offered, there began some polite conversation between the envious and the covetous man about which one would make the request. For the covetous man would not agree to ask for the gift, because he wanted to have for himself the double of his fellow's request. And when the envious man saw that, he wanted to ensure that his fellow would gain little good from the doubling of his petition. So immediately he requested for his part that he might have one of his eyes put out. By reason of that request, the envious man lost one eye, and the covetous man lost both.

Anger, the Offspring of Pride

Among the proud there are always contentions.

PROVERBS 13:10a, DOUAY-RHEIMS

MORNING READING

Wrath is undoubtedly another daughter of pride. No doubt wrath sometimes arises when a wrong is done to us, such as some harm to our person or loss of our goods. On such an occasion, because it often happens to us suddenly, the rule of reason may be hindered for awhile by the sudden shock of such an unexpected injury coming upon us unforeseen; for that reason, our sin in being angry is less serious. Nevertheless, you find in those who have made an evil habit of wrathfulness their nature, who seem more naturally disposed to anger and contrariness, that the very root of such vice is pride—even though their manner and behavior might be such that people would little know it. For no matter how simply they act, no matter how lowly they look, yet you will see them become testy at every slight provocation. They cannot abide one mere word that challenges them, they cannot bear to be contradicted in argument, but they fret and fume if their opinion is not accepted and their influence is not magnified.

Lord, curb my heart, forgive my guilt,
Make Thou my patience firmer;
For they must miss the good Thou wilt
Who at Thy chastenings murmur.

JOHANN MAJOR, 1613;
TRANSLATED BY CATHERINE WINKWORTH, 1863

FOR REFLECTION

"This deadly cancer of anger from which so much harm grows: It makes us unlike ourselves, makes us like timber wolves or furies from hell, drives us forth headlong upon the points of swords, makes us blindly run forth after other men's destruction as we hasten toward our own ruin." Lord, in what ways am I driven by anger to act unlovingly?

EVENING READING

From what does such contrariness arise in these habitually angry people, but from a secret cause of too high an opinion of themselves, so that it pierces their heart when they see any man esteem them less than they esteem themselves. Will you also perceive that an inflated estimation of ourselves is more than half the weight of our wrath? We will prove it to those who disagree. Take someone who reckons himself to be worthy of honor. Consider: Isn't he much more angry over one reproachful word of rebuke spoken to his face by someone he reckons to be only his equal or his inferior (such as perhaps a knave or beggar, in which case there is no great slander suffered) than he would be over the very same word spoken by someone whom he knows and acknowledges to be a great deal his better?

DAY 40

Esteeming Ourselves More Than God

You said in your heart, "I will ascend to heaven; above the stars of God I will set my throne on high ... I will make myself like the Most High."

ISAIAH 14:13-14

MORNING READING

The kind of good anger that we call holy zeal arises from the fact that we esteem our Lord God as we should—that we cannot help but be angry with those who esteem Him so little that they do not refrain from breaking His high commandments. In the same way, when we esteem ourselves quite highly, feelings of anger arise, so that our hearts are moved with ire and disdain against those who displease us, and who show by their behavior that they have less esteem for us than our proud heart expects. In this way, though we may not recognize it, yet indeed we reckon ourselves worthy of more reverence than we do God Himself alone.

When I survey the wondrous cross
On which the Prince of glory died
My richest gain I count but loss
And pour contempt on all my pride.

ISAAC WATTS, 1674–1748

FOR REFLECTION

"Give me, good Lord ... a love for You that is incomparably above my love for myself."

EVENING READING

I don't doubt that men will deny this. But would you like to see it proved to be so? Consider whether we are not more angry with one of our servants over the breach of one of our own commands, than we are with the breaching of all ten of God's commandments. Aren't we more angry over one insolent or spiteful word spoken against ourselves than with many blasphemous words irreverently spoken of God? And do you believe that we could be more angered by the diminishing of our own honor than that of God's honor, or expect to have our own commands better obeyed than God's, if we did not indeed esteem ourselves more than Him?

DAY 41

Proud and Foolish Covetousness

He who loves money will not be satisfied with money; nor he who loves wealth, with gain: this also is vanity.

ECCLESIASTES 5:10

MORNING READING

Covetousness is a sickness in which men are quite deceived. For it makes people seem to be something far different from what they truly are. The covetous may seem humble, yet they are very proud. They may seem wise, and yet they are very foolish. Consider their pride in the possession of goods: Whoever is well acquainted with them will well recognize how heartily they rejoice in daring to call "beggars" those who are better than they are. Why? Simply because money is not so abundant with those who value it less and spend it more liberally.

*Almighty Father, heav'n and earth with lavish wealth
   before Thee bow;
Those treasures owe to Thee their birth, Creator, Ruler,
   Giver, Thou.
The wealth of earth, of sky, of sea, the gold, the silver,
   sparkling gem,
The waving corn, the bending tree, are Thine;
   to us Thou lendest them.*

EDWARD A. DAYMAN, 1867

FOR REFLECTION

"Covetousness is like fire: the more wood that is fed to it, the more fervent and greedy it is." Do I have an acquisitive heart, Lord?

EVENING READING

Men think the greedy wise also, and they themselves agree, because they seem to be people with foresight who make provisions, not only for the present, but also for the time to come. But then they prove to be worse fools than those who live from hand to mouth. For the poor at least take some pleasure in what they have now, even though they may fare worse on another day. But these greedy misers pass the present time painfully because they are saving everything for some day in the future—thus they live on wretchedly, till all their days are past and there are none left to come. Then when they least expect it, all they have heaped up is left behind for strangers who can never thank them.

The Poverty of Covetousness

As he came from his mother's womb he shall go again, naked as he came, and shall take nothing for his toil, which he may carry away in his hand.

ECCLESIASTES 5:15

MORNING READING

The covetous may claim to be Christian, yet they have no trust in Christ. For they are always afraid of want in the time to come, no matter how much they have. Now I am utterly convinced that every man who has children is bound by the law of God and of nature to provide for them till they are at least able by the labor of their own hands to provide for their needs—though I don't think that God and nature expect much more than that, nor were we thrust out of the Paradise of pleasure to make us seek and long to be lords in this wretched earth. Nevertheless, it truly seems to me that no matter how little we have, if we are not content to be merry with it, but instead—to the discomfort, not only of ourselves, but of everyone around us—we live with whining and whimpering and heaviness of heart out of fear and dread of some want in the time to come, then plainly no matter how much we speak of faith and trust in Christ, we have in our hearts no more belief in His holy words nor trust in His faithful promise than an unbeliever.

Forbid it, Lord, that I should boast
Save in the death of Christ my God;
All the vain things that charm me most,
I sacrifice them to His blood.

ISAAC WATTS, 1674–1748

FOR REFLECTION

"This covetous gathering and miserly keeping of wealth, with all the delight that we take in beholding it, is only a very gay and golden dream, in which we imagine we have great riches; and in the sleep of this life we are glad and proud of it. But when death has once awakened us, our dream shall vanish, and of all the treasure that we only dreamed about, we shall not find one penny left in our hand." How should I be using my wealth today, Lord, since I may be gone tomorrow?

EVENING READING

These covetous folks who set their hearts on their hoards, and are proud when they look on their heaps of treasure, may reckon themselves rich, yet they are indeed quite wretched beggars. I mean those who are fully immersed in covetousness, who have all the characteristics that word implies—namely, that they are as loath to spend anything as they are glad to have everything. For they not only refuse to part with anything for the sake of liberality with others, but they also live wretchedly by withholding everything from themselves. And so they reckon themselves owners when they are in truth only mere keepers of other men's goods. For since they find it in their hearts to spend nothing upon themselves, but keep it all for the executors of their estates, even now they make it not their own because they won't use it. Already they have given it to other men for whose use and on whose behalf they keep it.

Gluttony, a Kind of Suicide

For the drunkard and the glutton will come to poverty, and drowsiness will clothe a man with rags.

PROVERBS 23:21

MORNING READING

If we see men die from famine in some year of scarcity, we consider it a serious matter: We march in processions, we pray for plenty, and we think the world is coming to an end. But in times of abundance, every year there are many people who die of gluttony. Yet we take no heed of that at all, and we blame the sickness for the death it caused, rather than blaming gluttony for the sickness it caused.

And if a man is killed by the sword, much is debated about the reason: the coroner examines, the inquest is made, the charges are made, the felon is arrested and indicted, the court proceeds, the felon is sent to his execution, and dies for his crime. Yet if men would examine how many are killed with weapons and how many eat and drink themselves to death, there would be found more dead from the cup and the kitchen than from the thrust of a sword. Yet no one says anything about that at all.

Lord Jesus, think on me
And purge away my sin;
From earth-born passions set me free
And make me pure within.

SYNESIUS OF CYRENE, 430;
TRANSLATED BY ALLEN W. CHATFIELD, 1876

FOR REFLECTION

"Through intemperate living we drive ourselves to sickness, and patch then ourselves up with medicine; but with a sober diet and temperance we might have less need of remedies and keep ourselves in health." Grant me temperance and self-control, Father.

EVENING READING

Now if a man should willingly kill himself with a knife, the world marvels at it; and if he is charged with his own death, his goods are forfeited and his corpse is cast out on a dunghill, with his body refused a Christian burial. Yet these gluttons daily kill themselves with their own hands—but no one finds fault with them. Instead, his corpse is carried into the church, and with much solemn ceremony the body is taken before the high altar and then buried—even though he has all his life (as the apostle says) made his belly his God, and known no other. In that way he has abused not only the name of Christian, preferring the joy of his belly over all the joys of heaven, but also abusing his nature and dignity as a rational creature. For while nature and reason show us that we should eat only to live, these gluttons are so glutted with the brutish pleasures of taste that they only wish to live in order to eat.

"A Simple Medicine…"

REMEMBERING OUR
FINAL DESTINY

Medicine for the Sin-Sick Soul

In all you do, remember the end of your life, and then you will never sin.

SIRACH 7:36

MORNING READING

The physician sends his prescription to the pharmacist, and in it he writes a costly recipe of many strange herbs and roots, fetched from faraway countries—sometimes including drugs that have long lain unused, so that they are no longer potent; or perhaps they can't be obtained at all. But this divine Physician sends his prescription for your sick soul not to some pharmacist, but to you yourself, with no exotic ingredients, nothing costly to buy, nothing to be fetched from far away. Instead, all its ingredients can be gathered any time of the year in the garden of your own soul. Let us hear, then, what wholesome recipe this is: Remember your last days, says this biblical prescription, and you will never sin in this world.

Great God, what do I see and hear? The end of things created;
The Judge of mankind doth appear on clouds of glory seated.
The trumpet sounds; the graves restore
The dead which they contained before:
Prepare, my soul, to meet Him.

AUTHOR UNKNOWN

"Here is a simple medicine, containing only four herbs, common and well-known—namely, death, judgment day, pain, and joy." How often do I take my spiritual medicine, Lord?

EVENING READING

For what would a man give for a sure medicine, that was of such strength that it would keep him from sickness all his life, so that by avoiding sickness in this way he could be sure to continue his life for a hundred years? In the same way, these biblical words give us all a sure medicine, if we don't neglect to receive them, by which we can keep from sickness: not sickness of the body—which no health can long keep from death, for die we must in a few years, no matter how long we live—but of the soul, which if preserved in this life from the sickness of sin, shall afterward live eternally in joy, and be preserved from the living death of everlasting pain.

Sickness Is Never Far Away

Have pity on me, O Lord, for I am languishing; heal me, O Lord, for my body is in terror; My soul, too, is utterly terrified…. For among the dead no one remembers you.

PSALM 6:3, 6 NAB

MORNING READING

Now then if you were ever sick, especially of a dreaded disease, wouldn't you—if you knew your condition—have a better remembrance of death than you do now? Perhaps it would be hard to make you believe that you were sick as long as you felt no pain, and yet the absence of such symptoms is no guarantee of health. Don't you know that many a man is infected with a serious sickness a good while before he recognizes it, and his body grievously damaged within before he ever feels discomfort? How many men have there been, who have walked around as men marked by God for death, never perceiving themselves to be sick, but as merry as ever they were in their lives—until others gave them warning how near they were to death? Therefore, never reckon yourself healthy even when you feel no pain.

Choose, Lord, for me my friends, my sickness or my health;
Choose Thou my cares for me, my poverty or wealth.
Not mine, not mine the choice in things both great and small;
Be Thou my Guide, my Strength, my Wisdom, and my all.

HORATIUS BONAR, 1808–89

FOR REFLECTION

"When you go forth from this world in death, who will go with you? Won't even your own flesh let you walk away, a naked, helpless soul?" Be with me in health and in sickness, in life and in death, Jesus.

EVENING READING

You would remember death with somewhat more effect, and more clearly recognize his nearness, if you knew yourself to be sick—especially with a dreaded illness that was fatal, even if you didn't yet feel much pain. For commonly, when we are sick, then we begin truly to know ourselves; then pain brings us home to ourselves; then we think how merry a thing it would be to pray in good health, though we can't do that now because of our grief. Then we care little for all our gay belongings; then we desire no delicate luxuries. And as for Lady Lechery, then we abhor even the thought of her. Then we think within ourselves, that if ever we recover and mend in body, we will amend in soul, leave all vices, and be virtuously occupied for the rest of our life. For that reason, we should be, when we are healthy, as we think we would be when we are sick.

Our Frail Bodies

The spirit indeed is willing, but the flesh is weak.

MATTHEW 26:41

MORNING READING

Now then I ask you to consider: Our bodies are ever so weak in themselves that if we didn't wrap them up continually in warm clothes, we wouldn't be able to survive one winter week. Consider how our bodies have so serious a sickness and such a continual consumption within themselves that even the strongest wouldn't be able to endure and continue for ten straight days were it not that once or twice a day we're obliged to take medicines inside them to patch them up clumsily and keep them as long as we can. For what is our food and drink but medicines against hunger and thirst, that give us warning of what we lose daily by our inward consumption? And despite all the medicines we use, we shall die in the end from that consumption, even if we never suffer any other sickness.

All men living are but mortal; yea, all flesh must fade as grass;
Only through death's gloomy portal to eternal life we pass.
This frail body here must perish ere the heavenly joys it cherish.

JOHANN G. ALBINUS, 1652;
TRANSLATED BY CATHERINE WINKWORTH, 1863

FOR REFLECTION

"For as the flame is close to the smoke, so death is close to an incurable sickness—and such is all our life." Let me be humbled by the frailty of my life, Lord.

EVENING READING

Consider also that despite all our swaddling and tending to ourselves with warm clothes, and daily "medicines" of food and drink, yet our bodies can't bear to live without being obliged to spend half our time in every twenty-four hours fallen in a swoon that we call sleep. And there we lie like dead sticks for a long time before we come to ourselves again—so that among all the wise men of old, it was agreed that sleep is the very image of death.

Thus you may surely see, that all our whole life is but a sickness without remedy, an incurable corruption. And despite all our wrapping and plastering, bandaged up to live as long as we can, in the end we undoubtedly die of that same sickness, even though another illness may never come along. So, then, if you consider this reality well, you will look upon death not as a stranger, but as a close neighbor.

Born to Die

In your book they are all written; my days were limited before one of them existed.

PSALM 139:16b NAB

MORNING READING

We die all the while we are living. For what is dying? Is it anything other than the passage and going out of this present life? Consider this parallel: If you are going out of a house, at what point are you going out: only when your foot is on the farthest edge of the threshold and your body is halfway out the door? Or are you going out when you begin to set the first foot forward to go out, wherever you might be standing in the house as you begin your journey? I would say that you are going out of the house from the very first foot you set forward to go forth. And if someone were coming here to this town, he would be coming here not only as he was entering at the town gate, but also as he went the entire way from the place where he started. And surely I think that in the same way, a man is not only dying—that is to say, going his way out of this life—while he lies gasping for breath, but also all the while that he is going toward his end. And that includes the whole span of his life, from the first moment until the last is finished.

In the midst of earthly life snares of death surround us;
Who shall help us in the strife, lest the foe confound us?
Thou only, Lord, Thou only!
We mourn that we have greatly erred,
That our sins Thy wrath have stirred.
Eternal Lord God, save us lest we perish in the bitter pangs of
    death!

MARTIN LUTHER, 1524

FOR REFLECTION

"We should never look at death as something far off; for even if
he seems to be in no hurry toward us, yet we ourselves never
cease to hurry toward him." Am I ready to meet You at any
time, Lord?

EVENING READING

Now if this be the case, as it seems to me that reason proves,
then a man is always dying from before his birth, and every
hour of our age as it passes by, cuts its own length out of our
life, and makes it shorter by that much, and our death so much
the nearer. Thus the measuring of time and diminishing of life,
as we approach death, is nothing else but from our beginning
to our ending one continual dying. In whatever way we live—
whether we wake or sleep, we eat or drink, we mourn or
sing—all the while we are dying.

Youth Is No Defense Against Death

Remember also your Creator in the days of your youth, before the evil days come, and ... the dust returns to the earth as it was, and the spirit returns to God who gave it.

ECCLESIASTES 12:1, 7

MORNING READING

If you are a young man, and think that your death is far off, because by nature you likely have many years to live, then consider this: Suppose there are two men both condemned to death, and both carried out in a cart at the same time for execution. One of the two is sure that the place of his execution is only a mile away; the other knows that he must be carried one hundred miles to his execution. The one in the cart to be carried a hundred miles will not take much more pleasure than his fellow in the length of his journey, notwithstanding the fact that it is a hundred times longer than his fellow's, and that he thus has for that reason a hundred times longer to live. For it is sure and beyond all question that he will still die at the end.

Now reckon yourself a young man in your best vigor—say, twenty years of age. Let there be another man, ninety years old. Both of you must die; both of you are in the cart being carried forward. His gallows and death stand within ten miles at the farthest, and yours within eighty. I don't see why you should think less of your death than he, even though your way is longer, since you are sure you will never cease riding till you come to it.

Who knows when death may overtake me? Time passes on, my end draws near.

How swiftly can my breath forsake me! How soon can life's last
  hour appear!
My God, for Jesus' sake I pray Thy peace may bless my dying
  day.

EMILIE JULIANE, 1686

FOR REFLECTION

"Behold death, and ponder him as he is, and in this way take
the opportunity to flee vain pleasures of the flesh that keep out
the true pleasures of the soul." Lord, have I allowed youth to
give me a false sense of security?

EVENING READING

In our example, you are certain to be riding toward death even
if you are sure that the place of your execution stands far beyond that of your fellow. But what if there are two roads to the
place of your execution: one, eighty miles farther than that of
your fellow; the other, five miles nearer than his? When you
are put in the cart, you are warned about both roads; and
though you are shown that it is more likely you will be carried
the longer way, yet it might happen that you will go the
shorter—and you will never know which way you will be carried until you come to the place of your execution.

Now all of us are in this situation. For our Lord has not told
us His intentions about the time of our death. Therefore, if
you will consider how little reason you have to reckon your
death far off, merely because of your youth, then reckon how
many who were as young as you have died on the very same
road on which you ride. How many have been drowned in the
very same waters in which you row? And thus shall you well
see, that you have no cause to look upon your death as a thing
far off, but rather as a thing undoubtedly near you, and ever
walking with you.

An Antidote to Pride

Pride goes before destruction, and a haughty spirit before a fall.

PROVERBS 16:18

MORNING READING

Young and old, man and woman, rich and poor, prince and page, all the while we live in this world are but prisoners, and are in a sure prison from which no one can escape. And we are in a worse situation than those who are apprehended and imprisoned for theft. For they, even if their hearts listen with heaviness to the judge's verdict, yet have some hope either to break out of prison, or to escape there by someone's favor, or to receive pardon after their condemnation. But our plight is otherwise: We are all very sure that we are condemned to death of one sort or another; and though we don't know which kind of death will be ours, yet we can all tell that we will die. And clearly we know that we can in no way be pardoned of this death sentence—for the King by whose high sentence we are condemned to die would not pardon even His own Son of this death. As for escaping, no man can expect that. The prison is large with many prisoners in it, but the Jailer can lose none of them: He is present in every place, and there is no corner into which we can creep out of His sight.

We are still as in a dungeon living, still oppressed with sorrow and misgiving;
Our undertakings are but toils and troubles and heart

breakings.
Come, O Christ, and loose the chains that bind us.
Lead us forth, and cast this world behind us.

SIMON DACH, 1635;
TRANSLATED BY HENRY WADSWORTH LONGFELLOW

FOR REFLECTION

"Almighty Jesus, my sweet Savior, who would condescend with Your own almighty hands to wash the feet of Your twelve apostles ... grant through Your excellent goodness to wash the filthy feet of my inclinations in such a way that pride will not enter into my heart."

EVENING READING

There is no remedy for it then. As condemned folk and convicts, in this prison of the earth we carry on awhile.... Till suddenly, though it is the last thing we are expecting, it happens: Young, old, poor and rich, merry and sad, prince, page, pope, and poor soul priest, now one, now another, sometimes a great crowd at once, without any particular order, without respect to age or estate, all stripped stark naked and laid out on a sheet, they are put to death in different ways in some corner of the same prison....

Now come forth, you proud prisoner, for assuredly you are no better, no matter how high and mighty you look. When you build in prison a palace for your descendants, isn't it a great vainglory for such a work to be well thought of? You build the tower of Babel in a corner of the prison and are very proud of it: But sometime the Jailer will beat it down again with shame.... You are proud of the arms of your ancestors displayed in the prison: and all your pride comes because you forget that it is a prison.

DAY 50

A Cure for Envy

*But, as for me, I almost lost my balance; my feet all but slipped,
Because I was envious of the arrogant when I saw them prosper
though they were wicked.... Though I tried to understand this
it seemed to me too difficult, Till I entered the sanctuary of
God and considered their final destiny.*

PSALM 73:2-3, 16-17 NAB

MORNING READING

Envy is the daughter of pride, as Saint Augustine says; strangle
the mother and you will destroy the daughter. So keep in mind
that the same remembrance of death which serves as medicine
against the pestilent, swelling sore of pride provides also the
remedy for the venomous vice of envy. For the one who envies
another person does so for the sake of something that person
possesses which would make him proud if he had it himself.

The considerations about death that we have spoken about
before as a way to repress pride will make you set little value on
such things, whether you possess them or someone else does.
It follows, then, that the same considerations about death will
leave you little reason to envy such things in anyone else, for
they will possess them for only a brief season. You would not,
for shame, have men think you so mad as to envy a poor soul
for playing the role of a lord one night in a play. And could you
envy a perpetually sick man, a man who carries his death
wound with him, a man who is but a prisoner condemned to
death, a man who is in the executioner's cart already being carried to the gallows?

Then woe to those who scorned the Lord and sought but carnal
  pleasures,
Who here despised His precious word and envied earthly trea-
  sures!
With shame and trembling they will stand
And at the Judge's stern command
To Satan be delivered.

BARTHOLOMAEUS RINGWALDT, 1586;
TRANSLATED BY PHILIP A. PETER, 1880

FOR REFLECTION

"If we were to ... esteem everything according to its true nature, rather than according to men's false opinion, then we
would never see any reason to envy any man, but rather we
would pity every man—and pity those most who have the
most to be envied for, since they are the ones who will shortly
lose the most." Father, do I envy or pity those who have so
much to lose?

EVENING READING

Since men commonly envy their betters, the remembrance of
death should according to reason be a great remedy for that
vice. For I suppose that even if there were someone in a position far above you, you would not greatly envy his estate if you
thought that you might be his equal the next week. So why
should you, then, envy him now, seeing that death may make
you both equals tomorrow night, and will undoubtedly do so
within a few years? We are certain that death will take away all
that we envy any man for—and even if we are uncertain how
soon, yet we are very sure that it will not be long.

A Remedy for Anger

Give up your anger, and forsake wrath; be not vexed, it will only harm you. For evildoers shall be cut off.... Yet a little while, and the wicked man shall be no more.

PSALM 37:8-10 NAB

MORNING READING

If remembering death can restrain our pride, we should apply the same remedy to anger. For who could be angry over the loss of goods if he remembers well how short a time he gets to keep them in the first place—how soon death might take them from him? Who could esteem himself so highly that he would take to heart a vile rebuke spoken to his face if he remembered who he really is: a poor prisoner condemned to death? Or how could we become so angry as we do now whenever someone does us bodily injury, if we were to think deeply about how we are indeed already laid in the executioner's cart? If we consider that this life is only a pilgrimage, and that we have no permanent dwelling place here, how foolish it is to scold and fight over little things along the way!

*My end to ponder, teach me ever
And, ere the hour of death appears,
To cast my soul on Christ my Savior,
Nor spare repentant sighs and tears.*

EMILIE JULIANE, 1686

FOR REFLECTION

"Almighty Jesus Christ ... give us Your grace so that we may ... reckon ourselves, not as dwellers, but as pilgrims on earth, so that we may hurry, walking with faith along the way of virtuous works, and longing to come to the glorious country where You have bought us an inheritance forever with Your own precious blood."

EVENING READING

If we should see two men fighting together over serious matters, we would still think them both crazy if they did not leave off fighting when they saw a ferocious lion coming toward them, ready to devour them both. Now considering that we surely see that death is coming on us all, and will undoubtedly within a short time devour us all—how soon, we don't know—isn't it worse than insanity to be angry and bear malice to one another, more often than not over trivial matters, in the same way children fight over cherry stones?

The Price of Gluttony and Drunkenness

And take heed to yourselves, lest perhaps your hearts be over-charged with surfeiting and drunkenness, and the cares of this life, and that day come upon you suddenly.

LUKE 21:34 DOUAY-RHEIMS

MORNING READING

If God never punished gluttony, yet it would bring with itself punishment enough: It disfigures the face, discolors the skin, and mars the shape of the body. It makes the body fat and flabby, the face drowsy, the nose droopy, the mouth spitting, the eyes blurred, the teeth rotten, the breath stinking, the hands trembling, the head hanging, and the feet tottering. In the end, it leaves no part of the body in its right function and frame. And beside the daily dullness and grief that the unwieldy body feels, by the stuffing of its paunch so full, it brings in by degrees swelling, colic, stones, painful urination, gout, cramps, palsy, sores, pestilence, and apoplexy—disease and sickness of such kind that either will soon destroy us or, worse yet, keep us in such pain and torment that the longer we live, the more wretched we are.

The world that smiled when morn was breaking
May change for me e'er close of day;
For while on earth my home I'm making
Death's threat is never far away.

EMILIE JULIANE, 1686

FOR REFLECTION

"What a wonder it is that the world is so mad we would rather have sin with pain than virtue with pleasure!" What price am I paying for my sins, Lord?

EVENING READING

Now gluttons should remember and think upon the painful time of death, in which the hand will not be able to feed the mouth; and the mouth that used to guzzle by the gallon, and cram in the meat by the handfuls, will hardly be able to take in three drops with a spoon without spitting it out again. Often they have had a hangover and slept themselves sober. But then they will feel a swimming and aching in their drunken head, when the daze of death will keep all sweet sleep out of their watery eyes. Often have they fallen in the mire and had to be carried from there to bed. But now they will fall in the bed, and from there be laid and left in the mire, until Gabriel wakes them with his trumpet.

If these intemperate people would well remember that their manner of living will hasten this dreadful day, I truly think it would not fail to make them more moderate in their living so that they would utterly flee such outrageously riotous and deadly excess.

"This Weeping World..."

MERRY IN TRIBULATION

DAY 53
Our Need for Tribulation

"My son, do not regard lightly the discipline of the Lord, nor lose courage when you are punished by him. For the Lord disciplines him whom he loves, and chastises every son whom he receives." It is for discipline that you have to endure. God is treating you as sons.

HEBREWS 12:5-7

MORNING READING

Tribulation is a gracious gift from God—one that He especially gives His special friends. It is a thing that in Scripture is highly commended and praised; a thing that we are spared for long only to our peril; a thing that, if not sent by God to us, we must seek and undergo by our own penance; a thing that helps to purge the sins of our past; a thing that preserves us from sins that otherwise would come; a thing that causes us to hold the world in less esteem; a thing that inspires us to draw closer to God; a thing that diminishes considerably our pain in purgatory; a thing that considerably increases our final reward in heaven; the thing by which our Savior entered His own kingdom; the thing with which all His apostles followed Him there; the thing that our Savior exhorts all men to embrace; the thing without which, He says, we are not His disciples; the thing without which no man can get to heaven.

Ye fearful saints, fresh courage take; the clouds ye so much dread
Are big with mercy and shall break in blessings on your head.
Judge not the Lord by feeble sense, but trust Him for His grace;
Behind a frowning Providence he hides a smiling face.

WILLIAM COWPER, 1731–1800

FOR REFLECTION

"In this short season of sowing in this weeping world, we must water our seed with the showers of our tears—and then we will have in heaven a merry, laughing harvest forever." Father, in every sadness, help me make my tears a gift to You.

EVENING READING

Alas, silly souls, what reason is there to envy those who are always wealthy in this world and always escaping tribulation? Would we, who are servants, expect more privilege in our Master's house than our Master had himself? Would we enter His kingdom with ease when He Himself did not enter His own kingdom without pain? We cannot have continual wealth both in this world and in the next as well. Therefore, those who are in this world without any tribulation, who enjoy a long, continual course of uninterrupted prosperity, have good cause for fear and discomfort. Those whom God never sends tribulation may well have fallen far out of His favor and be standing deep in His indignation and displeasure—for He tends to send tribulation to those He loves. On the other hand, those who have tribulation have good reason to take great inward comfort and spiritual consolation in the midst of their great grief.

Trusting God's Wisdom

*Then Job answered the Lord and said "I know that you can do
all things, and that no purpose of yours can be hindered. I have
dealt with great things that I do not understand; things too
wonderful for me, which I cannot know."*

JOB 42:1-3 NAB

MORNING READING

For it is almost a common thing among men to speak sometimes as if they would like to change the works of God. And I
think there are few men—though they dare not be so bold to
admit it—who don't imagine that if they had been God's advi-
sor in the creation of the world, they could have made it better.
And if they had been put in charge of the process, they would
have had God change the way He made many things.

Yet for all that, if God were to take us all on as advisors now,
and change nothing until we had all agreed upon it, I think the
world would quite likely go on as it already does till doomsday.
But you never know: We might all agree, at least, to be given
wings!

*What God ordains is always good, this truth remains un-
shaken.*
Though sorrow, need or death be mine, I shall not be forsaken.
I fear no harm, for with His arm
He shall embrace and shield me.
So to my God I yield me.

SAMUEL RODIGAST, 1649–1708

FOR REFLECTION

"When the time is right, God brings forth all things from the secret treasure chest of His wisdom." Father, I trust You to work all things together for my good.

EVENING READING

Let no man interpret his own trouble or sickness as a sign of God's hatred—unless he feels himself resentful about it, and impatient, and discontent with his condition. For in that case, it does indeed become a sign of divine wrath and vengeance, and to the sufferer, such adversity becomes just as fruitless as it is painful. The effect of it will be nothing else than the beginning of his hell here on earth. But on the other hand, if he takes it all patiently, it purges him; if he suffers it gladly, then it will merit him a great deal. For that reason, glad may the man be who with meekness welcomes God's chastisement.

Praying in Tribulation

And going a little farther [Jesus] fell on his face and prayed, "My Father, if it be possible, let this cup pass from me; nevertheless, not as I will, but as thou wilt."

MATTHEW 26:39

MORNING READING

Tribulations are of various sorts, and some of these a man may ask God to take from him, and find comfort in the confidence that God will do so. Therefore, against hunger, sickness and bodily harm, and against the loss of either body or soul, men may often legitimately pray for God's goodness either for themselves or for a friend. For this purpose many devout prayers are included in the common services of our Holy Mother Church. And for our help in some of these matters some of the petitions in the Our Father serve well, in which we pray daily for our daily food, and to be kept from temptation, and to be delivered from evil.

*Nearer, my God, to Thee, nearer to Thee!
E'en though it be a cross that raiseth me;
Still all my song shall be, nearer, my God, to Thee.*

SARAH F. ADAMS, 1805–48

FOR REFLECTION

"So blind are we in this mortal life, and so unaware of what will happen—so uncertain even of how we will think tomorrow—that God could not take vengeance on a man more easily in this world than by granting his own foolish wishes." Grant me, Father, not what I plead for, but what You know is best for me.

EVENING READING

For the salvation of our soul we may boldly pray. For grace we may pray boldly as well, for faith, for hope and for love, and for every virtue that will serve to lead us to heaven. But as for all other matters, including our dealings with tribulation, we may never rightly pray specifically for something without expressing or at least implying one condition: that is, that if God sees that the contrary is better for us, we will trust the matter to His whole will. Then, instead of praying that He will take away our grief, we will pray that God in His goodness may send us either spiritual comfort to endure it gladly, or at least strength to bear it patiently. For if we determine on our own that we will take no comfort in anything but deliverance from our tribulation, then we are either dictating to God that we insist He must not do something better for us—even though He would—than we ourselves will allow. Or else we are declaring that we ourselves can tell better than He can what is best for us.

Rejoicing in Adversity

The Lord gave, and the Lord has taken away; blessed be the name of the Lord.

JOB 1:21b

MORNING READING

[*From a letter to his wife.*] I have been informed by my son of the loss of our barns by fire and those of our neighbors as well, along with all the grain that was stored there. Even though, apart from God's will, it was a great pity to have so much good grain lost, since it has pleased Him to send us this incident, we must and are bound not only to be content with what he has sent us, but also glad about it. He sent us in the first place all that we have lost, and since He has by these circumstances taken it away again, so that His pleasure may be fulfilled, let us never begrudge it. Instead, let us take it in stride and thank Him heartily for adversity as well as for prosperity.

O Joy that seekest me through pain,
I cannot close my heart to Thee;
I trace the rainbow through the rain
And feel the promise is not vain
That morn shall tearless be.

GEORGE MATHESON, 1842–1906

FOR REFLECTION

"I pray: God make you all merry in the hope of heaven."

EVENING READING

Perhaps we have more cause to thank God for our loss than for our gain, for His wisdom can see better what is good for us than we ourselves can see. Therefore I pray you, be of good cheer and take all the household with you to church, where you should thank God: both for what He has given us and for what He has left us—which, if it pleases Him, He can increase whenever He wants to. And if He chooses to leave us even less, then may it be His pleasure to do so. I pray you: With the children and with all the household, be merry in God.

Forgiving Our Enemies

*Repay no one evil for evil.... Beloved, never avenge yourselves,
but leave it to the wrath of God; for it is written, "Vengeance is
mine, I will repay, says the Lord."*

ROMANS 12:17, 19

MORNING READING

Bear no malice nor evil will to any living man. For the man is
either good or evil. If he is good, and I hate him, then I am
evil. If he is evil, then either he will repent and die good, and
go to God, or he will remain evil, and die evil, and go to the
devil. So then let me remember that if he is saved, and if I am
saved too (as I trust to be), then he will in heaven not fail to
love me quite heartily, and I shall then in the same way love
him.

Why then should I now hate someone for this little while on
earth who will in the hereafter love me forever? And why then
should I now be an enemy to someone with whom I will even-
tually be joined in eternal friendship? On the other hand, if he
should remain evil and be damned, then he is facing such an
outrageous, eternal sorrow that I would rightly think myself a
deadly cruel wretch if I would not now rather pity his pain
than speak evil of him.

Some will hate thee, some will love thee,
Some will flatter, some will slight;
Cease from man, and look above thee:
Trust in God, and do the right.

NORMAN MACLEOD, 1812–72

FOR REFLECTION

"Almighty God, have mercy on all who bear an evil will toward me, and who wish to harm me; by the kind of gentle, tender, merciful means that Your infinite wisdom can best devise, grant to correct and redress both their faults and mine together, and make us saved souls in heaven together, where we may ever live and love together with You and Your blessed saints."

EVENING READING

I counsel every good friend of mine: Unless you find yourself in such a place that your position of authority involves the duty to punish an evil man, then leave to God the desire to punish. Or else leave the responsibility of correction to those who are so grounded in charity, and hold so firmly to God, that no secret, malicious, cruel inclination, under the guise of a just and virtuous zeal, can creep in and sabotage their task. But those of us who are no better than men of an inferior sort should always pray for the kind of merciful repentance in other folks that our own conscience shows us we need ourselves.

The Church in Peril

And he came the third time, and said to them, "Are you still sleeping and taking your rest? It is enough; the hour has come; the Son of Man is betrayed into the hands of sinners. Rise, let us be going."

MARK 14:41-42a

MORNING READING

Whenever we see an imminent danger that the mystical body of Christ, the Church of Christ—that is, the Christian people—will be brought to ruin at the hands of wicked men, then we are right to fear that once again, the time approaches when "the Son of Man is to be handed over to sinners." Alas, for some centuries now we have not failed to see this happening somewhere, now in one place, now in another, while our cruel enemies invade some parts of the Christian dominion and other parts are torn in pieces by the internal strife of many heretical sects.

Whenever we see such things or hear that they are beginning to happen, however far away, let us consider that this is no time for us to sit and sleep. Rather, we must get up immediately and help in any way we can to relieve the danger others face—by our prayers at least, if in no other way. Nor is such danger to be taken lightly simply because it happens at some distance from us.

I love Thy Church, O God: Her walls before Thee stand,
Dear as the apple of Thine eye, and graven on Thy hand.
For her my tears shall fall; for her my prayers ascend;
To her my cares and toils be given till toils and cares shall end.

TIMOTHY DWIGHT, 1752–1817

FOR REFLECTION

"It can only be disgraceful for some Christians to snore while other Christians are in peril." Lord, have mercy on my brothers and sisters who this day are suffering for Your sake.

EVENING READING

If we are perhaps unmoved by the calamities of others simply because they are at some distance from us, let us at least be moved by our own danger. For we have reason to fear that the destructive force of the Church's enemies will make its way from them to us, just as we have learned from many examples how rapid the advancing force of a blaze can be and how terrifying is the contagion of a raging plague. Since, therefore, all human defenses are futile without the help of God to ward off such evils, let us always remember these words from the gospel and let us always imagine that Christ Himself is again speaking to us over and over those words of His: "Why are you sleeping? Get up and pray that you may not enter into temptation."

Whenever we hear, then, that such calamities have befallen other peoples, no matter how distant, let us immediately recall this command of Christ. For the fact is that wherever this plague of heresy spreads today most fiercely, everyone was not infected in a single day. Rather the contagion grows gradually and invisibly: Those who despise the false teachings at first, afterwards find themselves willing to bear and answer it with half-hearted scorn. Next they come to tolerate these wicked discussions, and finally they are swept away into error, until like a cancer (as the apostle says) the creeping disease finally takes over the whole country [see 2 Tm 2:17]. Therefore we must stay awake, get up, and pray constantly that all those who have fallen into this miserable folly through the wiles of Satan may quickly come to their senses—and that God may never allow us to enter into this kind of temptation.

God Will Triumph

Jesus said to the chief captains and officers of the temple and elders, who had come out against him "... This is your hour, and the power of darkness."

LUKE 22:52-53

MORNING READING

This, Jesus said to those who came to arrest Him, is the hour and the brief power of darkness. A man who walks in darkness does not know where he is going [see Jn 12:35]; nor do you see or know what you are doing. For that reason I Myself will pray that you may be forgiven for what you are plotting to do to Me [see Lk 23:34]. Yet not every man will be forgiven. Blindness will not be an excuse for everyone. For you yourselves create your own darkness. You extinguish the light. You blind your own eyes first, and then the eyes of others, so that you become the blind leading the blind who will both fall into a ditch [see Mt 15:14]. But this, your hour, is short.

Rise, God, judge Thou the earth in might, this wicked earth
*   redress;*
For Thou art He who shall by right the nations all possess.
For great Thou art, and wonders great by Thy strong hand are
*   done:*
Thou in Thy everlasting seat remainest God alone.

JOHN MILTON, 1608–74

FOR REFLECTION

"This present moment of darkness is only an instant of time that is forever caught between a past that has vanished and a future that has yet to arrive." Open my eyes in faith, Lord, to see beyond this present darkness.

EVENING READING

This hour and this power of darkness are not given to you now against Me only. Such an hour and such a brief power of darkness will be given as well in other times to other governors and other caesars against other disciples of Mine. And this too will truly be the power of darkness. For whatever My disciples endure and say, they will not endure and say by their own strength. Rather, overcoming through My strength they will win their souls by their patience [see Lk 21:19], and it is My Father's Spirit who will speak through them [see Mt 10:20].

In the same way, those who persecute and kill them will neither do nor speak anything in their own power. Instead, the prince of darkness, who is already coming and who has no power over Me [see Jn 14:30] will inject his poison in the breasts of these tyrants and torturers. Through them, he will prove and exert his power through them for the brief season allowed him. For that reason, My comrades-in-arms will be struggling not against flesh and blood, but against princes and powers, against the rulers of the darkness of this world, against the spiritual forces of evil in high places [see Eph 6:12]. But although the nations have raged and the people devised vain things [see Ps 2:1] God will cast all His enemies down before Him like a footstool beneath His feet [see Is 66:1].

Thoughts in the Shadow of the Scaffold

For his sake I have suffered the loss of all things, and count them as refuse, in order that I may gain Christ.

PHILIPPIANS 3:8b

MORNING READING

Give me Your grace, good Lord, to count the world as nothing; to set my mind firmly on You and not to hang on the blasting words of men's mouths; to be content to be solitary; not to long for worldly company; little and little to cast off the world utterly, and rid my mind of all the world's business; not to long to hear of any worldly things, but to find that hearing about worldly delusions is unpleasant to me; gladly to be thinking of God, arousing His pity as I call for His help; to lean on the comfort of God, to labor to love Him busily; to know my own baseness and wretchedness, to humble and make myself meek under the mighty hand of God; to bewail the sins of my past; to suffer adversity patiently in order to purge them; gladly to bear my purgatory here; to be joyful in tribulations; to walk the narrow way that leads to life, to bear the cross with Christ.

Be still, my soul: the Lord is on thy side;
Bear patiently the cross of grief or pain.
Leave to thy God to order and provide;
In every change He faithful will remain.
Be still, my soul; thy best, thy heavenly friend
Through thorny ways leads to a joyful end.

KATHARINA VON SCHLEGEL, 1697–?;
TRANSLATED BY JANE L. BORTHWICK, 1813–97

FOR REFLECTION

"Glorious God, from this time forward give me the grace, with little regard for the world, to set and fix firmly my heart upon You in such a way that I may say with Your blessed apostle Saint Paul, 'The world is crucified to me, and I to the world. For to me to live is Christ and to die is gain. I wish to be dissolved and be with Christ'" [Gal 6:14; Phil 1:21-23].

EVENING READING

To keep in mind the last judgment, to have ever before my eyes my death that is ever at hand; to make death no stranger to me, to foresee and consider the everlasting fire of hell; to pray for pardon before the judge comes, to have continually in mind the Passion that Christ suffered for me; to give Him thanks unceasingly for His benefits, to redeem the time that I have lost until now; to abstain from empty conversation, to avoid frivolous, foolish mirth and gladness; to cut off unnecessary recreations; to consider as nothing the loss of worldly goods, friends, liberty, life and all, for the sake of winning Christ; to think my greatest enemies my best friends; for the brothers of Joseph could never have done him so much good with their love and favor as they did him with their malice and hatred.

These attitudes are more to be desired of every man than all the treasure of all the princes and kings, Christian and heathen, even if it were gathered and laid together all upon one heap.

Abbreviations for Titles of Works Cited

APB	*The Answer to a Poisoned Book*
DCAT	*A Dialogue of Comfort Against Tribulation*
DCH	*A Dialogue Concerning Heresies*
IMP	*Instructions, Meditations and Prayers*
LB	*Letter to Bugenhagen*
LT	*The Last Things*
SC	*The Sadness of Christ*
SS	*Supplication of Souls*
TUP	*Treatise Upon the Passion*
TRBB	*Treatise to Receive the Blessed Body of Our Lord*

Notes

INTRODUCTION

1. Letter to Lady Alice More, Woodstock, 3 Sept [1529].
2. William Roper, *The Life of Sir Thomas More,* volume 36 of The Harvard Classics, Charles W. Eliot, ed. (New York: P.F. Collier & Son, 1910), 102.
3. R.W. Chambers, *Thomas More* (Ann Arbor, Mich.: University of Michigan Press, 1958), 349.
4. Chambers, 41, 347.
5. Chambers, 90.
6. Roper, 104.
7. DCAT, bk. I, ch. 13.

READINGS

1. APB, bk. I, ch. 7; DCAT, bk. I, ch. 15
2. DCH, bk. I, ch. 25; TUP, ch. 1
3. DCH, bk. I, ch. 25; TUP, ch. 3
4. DCH, bk. II, ch. 2
5. DCH, bk. I, ch. 23; Letter to William Gonell, At Court, 22 May [1518?]
6. IMP, "A Devout Prayer"; TRBB
7. DCAT, bk. II, introduction; LT, introduction
8. TRBB
9. TRBB
10. TRBB; IMP, "A Devout Prayer"
11. TRBB; IMP, "A Devout Prayer"
12. TUP, ch. 4, lecture 2; TRBB
13. IMP, "A Devout Prayer"; TRBB
14. IMP, "A Devout Prayer"; TRBB
15. DCAT, bk. III, ch. 29; SC
16. SC; TUP, Introduction, second point

17. SC; IMP, "A Devout Prayer"

18. SC; IMP, "A Devout Prayer"

19. SC; IMP, "A Devout Prayer"

20. SC

21. SC

22. SC; APB, bk. II, ch. 4; TUP, Introduction, first point

23. DCH, bk. II, ch. 8

24. DCH, bk. II, ch. 8

25. TUP, ch. 1, lecture 5; IMP, "A Devout Prayer"

26. TUP, ch. 3

27. DCH, bk. I, ch. 18; TUP, ch. 3

28. SS, bk. II; LB

29. TUP, ch. 3

30. DCH, bk. III, ch. 11

31. TUP, ch. 1, lecture 2

32. LT, introduction

33. SC

34. SC

35. TUP, Introduction, first point

36. TUP, Introduction, first point; Letter to Antonio Bonvisi, Tower of London, 1535

37. TUP, Introduction, first point

38. LT, "Of Envy"

39. LT, "Of Wrath"

40. LT, "Of Wrath"; IMP, "A Devout Prayer"

41. DCAT bk. II, ch. 21; LT, "Of Covetousness"

42. LT, "Of Covetousness"

43. LT, "Of Gluttony"

44. LT, introduction

45. TUP, ch. 1, lecture 5; LT, "The Remembrance of Death"

46. LT, "The Remembrance of Death"

47. LT, "The Remembrance of Death"

48. LT, "The Remembrance of Death"

49. TUP, ch. 3; LT, "Of Pride"

50. LT, "Of Envy"

51. LT, "Of Wrath"; TUP, ch. 2

52. LT, "Of Gluttony"; LT, "Of Covetousness"

53. DCAT, bk. I, chs. 21, 13

54. DCH, bk. I, ch. 25; DCH, bk. II, ch. 8; SC

55. DCAT, bk. I, chs. 6, 8

56. Letter to Lady Alice More, Woodstock, 3 Sept [1529]; Letter to Margaret Roper, Tower of London, [April–May? 1534]

57. IMP, "A Godly Instruction"; IMP, "A Devout Prayer"

58. SC

59. SC

60. IMP, "A Godly Meditation"